THE ABDUCTION OF NELLY DON

PATRICE WILLIAMS MARKS

CONTENTS

READER REVIEWS

"I hope you don't have much planned for the next few days, because as soon as I promised I would stop reading and go to bed, I would end up grabbing my iPad for just one more chapter..."
Kristen Torgerson

ABSOLUTELY POSITIVELY FABULOUS.
I have always been a big fan of true crime stories and this book was one of the very, very best. Once I started reading, I absolutely couldn't stop until it was over. Also, what an unexpected and completely mind-blowing conclusion. WOW. This is a definite must read.
-Goodreads Reviewer, chelepissbcglobal.net

"This story is better than fiction! Pour yourself a drink, light up a coffin stick, and curl up with this twisted historical tale, be ready you won't be able to set it down!"
DJ6UAL An Irish Girl's Blog

"Once you start, you won't be able to put it down. It's got everything: romance, memorable characters, political corruption,

gun-toting gangsters and just enough humor :) Definitely recommend it!"
Amazon Reviewer Megan

"I was unsure of this e-book at first, but within a few pages, I was hooked. I HAD to know what would happen to Nelly, would she escape?"
Nicole Kaukinen "MommaKauk"

"The Abduction of Nelly Don is one of those rare books that had me intrigued from beginning to end. The story is very well written with just the right amount of crime, mystery, and suspense that had me glued to it as I turned each page."
Monica G - Top 1000 Reviewer

To my beloved sister, Phyllis and my furry babies Amore' and Cody.

STAND-ALONE HISTORICAL
THRILLER BOOK 1

The year is 1937 and England's well-respected investigator, Montgomery Vale is aboard the **Hindenburg**, determined to find answers about his family's mysterious past. But, an even more disturbing mystery derails him along the way.

FOR MORE INFORMATION, including links to all bookstores, CLICK HERE.

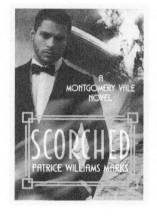

WHITE ANEMONES

*D*o you know what happens to the human body when it plummets over two hundred feet and makes contact with a body of water? Binding kinetic energy swirls between the two forces, man and water. Once they collide, the body will become more fluid, while the water remains and behaves the same. What is the result? It all depends on the point of contact.

Brook Hart, a handsome young man of 22, had no reason to consider such things as he lived a carefree life working for his father, Alex J. Hart, in one of their family-owned retail stores. The youngest of a brood of siblings, Brook was his father's favorite. His ambition and leadership skills put him first in line to take over the profitable family business.

Although the Great Depression was in full swing, the Harts were living the American Dream. That was until that fateful day.

. . .

"My father, please contact him... He will give you..."

Before Brook could finish his sentence, a terra-cotta brick, taken from a construction site on Hoover Street, knocked him to the ground.

"You people are *always* givin' orders," said Jack, a common hood, now wearing Hart's new waistcoat. Jack was a man beaten down by his own ineptness; a man who blamed the world for his continual failures. "Tired of the likes of you and your kind dinin' on deviled eggs, while I gotta steal a lousy loaf."

Jack and his accomplice, Thurmond, wrapped baling wire around Brook's legs and hands. The baling wire cut through the fine twill-cuffed trousers and butterfly-collared shirt, gouging Brook's flesh.

Jack said, "We ain't figured out where to stash ya during the negotiations, so we figured we'd hide ya in the San Mateo. Sorry, crumb, but this is your big kiss-off."

Thurmond echoed his sentiments, "Last kiss-off, friend."

Brook mumbled a few incoherent words as Jack took hold of the upper part of him, while Thurmond grabbed him from his knees down. They lifted him onto the railing of the San Mateo Bridge before heaving him over the side. Brook's wails reverberated over the river. He plunged into the water, feet first, and bobbed as he came up for air, unaware that hitting the water in this manner allows for a greater survival rate. Brook managed to free himself from the baling wire while thrashing about.

But Jack and Thurmond weren't through with Brook. "Look at 'im, making me work for a livin'." Jack walked to the back of his ten-year-old Hillman Tourer and unlocked the trunk. He reached inside, revealed a worn Thompson machine gun wrapped in yesterday's paper, walked over to the edge, climbed down onto the stringers, and aimed. Loud bursts in succession, "RAT A TAT TAT TAT TAT TAT TAT TAT TAT," then a pause, followed by thirteen more. "RAT A TAT TAT TAT TAT TAT TAT TAT TAT TAT TAT TAT TAT." Brook's body continued to convulse from the bullets long after he took his last breath. His body unhurriedly slipped below the surface.

Jack climbed back up, "Geez, almost forgot." Jack reached in the passenger side of the Tourer and pulled out a rumpled bag filled with white anemone flowers; a cup-shaped bloom known for its distinctive deep-lobed foliage. He tossed them to Thurmond as he shoved the Thompson back into the trunk.

Thurmond palmed a handful, scattered them at his feet, and kicked a few over the edge. While working at a nursery, the only legit job Jack held, he learned that this flower signified sorrow and death. This bit of information proved so appealing to Jack that he made it a point to remember.

The anemones danced and swirled as the wind's sudden gust blew open their petals, the same wind which would eventually scatter the spiritless petals far and away. Jack slammed the trunk shut. Both men climbed into the car and drove away.

These same white anemone flowers were left on the doorstep of Mr. and Mrs. Hart, along with a ransom note demanding forty-thousand dollars. Alex Hart paid the ransom, in hopes that his son would be returned to him. This was at the urging of police and their dear friend and champion, Senator James A. Reed.

His colleagues considered Senator Reed to be a member of the 'old right,' an 'isolationist.' But he'd assure you that he was neither old nor right. He considered himself progressive: someone who didn't always toe the Democratic Party line, not if it was used as a noose. The Phrasemaker himself, Woodrow Wilson, and Reed had often butted heads simply because it was a Tuesday.

Senator Reed once stood front and center on the Senate floor, denouncing the League of Nations as an H. G. Wells, 'One World of Brothers United in a League' as 'fanciful' and 'absurd.' Through this same electrified speech, he denounced his colleagues who ushered in Prohibition by calling them gentlemen who 'vote dry and drink wet.'

When meeting Reed, no smile would grace his face, yet his manner was always courteous. His gray eyes were penetrating, but were nothing but thoughtful. If you were a person with dishonorable intentions, your eyes would refuse to meet his. And if you wanted justice, you would see Senator Reed.

The senator frequently used the power behind his overpowering presence and office to quickly hastily resolve any desperate situation.

He met with the local police and pored over the evidence, including the ransom note and anemone flowers left behind on the bridge. A man of great faith in the system and even stronger fortitude, Reed's involvement kept the Hart kidnapping case front and center. Reed was not used to losing but had to accept this painful exception once young Brook Hart's remains surfaced.

His fortitude would be tested yet again, just seven months later, when Nell Donnelly was taken just outside her home.

A PORTRAIT

*B*orn Ellen Quinlan in 1889, Nelly, as her sisters were quick to call her, was the twelfth of thirteen children born on a rural farm in Kansas. Even among an infestation of children, Nelly stood out for her fearlessness.

Once following a creek along its winding path, Nelly was adamant about getting to the other side quicker than walking the two-mile trek around.

"You ain't gonna do it," Nelly's older, and thought-to-be-more-practical by all, sister Dot proclaimed. "That 'ole tree trunk can't hold but twenty-five pounds. You're about eighty-five, I reckon."

"You afraid?" Nelly taunted.

. . .

"Of course I am, Nelly. And if you had any brains, you would be, too."

Nelly bent down and fastened the buttons on her shoes before placing her right foot on the rotten log. She struggled to dislodge it with her foot, but she was unsuccessful. "This is much sturdier than that diseased elm." Nelly stood up on the log, still on land.

Dot shook her head and folded her arms. She pointed out, "You see that river rushin'?"

"It ain't a river, Dot. It's a creek."

"It's runnin' water, Nelly; runnin' faster than the likes of you. If you fall in, I ain't jumpin' in this time."

Nelly ignored the warnings and put one foot in front of the other, with arms outstretched for balance.

"See?" Nelly said proudly as she inched her way over the unbridled rivulet.

An exasperated Dot bellowed, "You're gonna die."

"No I ain't; just watch," Nelly assured her.

. . .

Nelly, feeling more confident, took bigger steps. She had the opposite bank in her sights. One step in front of the other... until she approached a clump of bracket fungi growing dead-center on the log. Orange, green, and brown growths fanned out. Nelly called to Dot, "Looks like a turkey tail." Nelly carefully stepped over the fungi and onto slippery green moss. She lost her footing and plunged into the frigid whitewater.

An overly excited Dot jumped up and down. "I told you. I told you." Dot kicked her shoes off and stepped onto the log, intent on reaching her sister.

Nelly flailed her arms before grasping a thin branch. She used the branch as a rope and pulled herself towards the log, though exhausted by the opposing currents. Dot was halfway there when Nelly managed to swing one leg over the trunk, pull herself up, and straddle the log. She steadied herself and rose with arms outstretched once again. "Don't gum up the works, Dot."

Dot angrily, with hands on hips, turned around and made her way back. Nelly stared down the bracket fungi. It was a showdown. Nelly shuffled towards the genesis of her failure, ambushed it with the toe of her soggy black and white, button-top leather doll shoes. Once it was sufficiently anni-hilated, she continued on, unobstructed, making it to the other side.

. . .

Nelly was also not one to come in second willingly. Being the twelfth child, she had grown weary of hand-me-downs. So from an early age, she became self-taught as a seamstress, making clothing not only for herself, but for her siblings as well.

On many occasions, Dot was known to say, "Nelly, if I do your chores for a week, can you make me a frilly frock?" For Dot knew that a simple "please" or one day of chores would not suffice, as Nelly had become a master negotiator before she reached puberty.

"Chores for a week *and* sixty-five cents."

"Sixty-five cents?" Dot exclaimed.

"I'll add pleats for comfort and adjustable sleeves."

"Nelly, you know I can go into town and pick one up for sixty-nine cents."

"The Mother Hubbard-looking ones shaped like a sack? Go ahead."

Dot pivoted on her heels and exited the room. Moments later, Dot returned, opened her coin purse, and counted out sixty-five cents.

. . .

As a teen, Nelly was not a classic beauty. She refused to stain her hair yellow like all the other young girls did. She also had a rather firm chin like her father. She inherited fawn eyes from her mother's side of the family. What she lacked in classic features, she more than made up for in determination, a fact not lost on her many suitors, who ranged from eager farm hands to college men home on break.

One such suitor was Walter Winkle; a tall, lanky redhead known for beating around the bush to such an extent that other ladies grew tired of guessing his intentions. Not Nelly. She did not care about his intentions, as she had intentions of her own that did not involve Walter.

After her high school graduation ceremony, Walter asked Nelly if he could have the pleasure of taking her home. She nodded in agreement. The entire thirty-minute dusty, bumpy ride home in his father's two-seater Shawmut Runabout, an open-aired roadster known for its simplicity, Walter worked up his courage to ask Nelly for her hand in marriage. However, when they reached their destination, Nelly surged from the vehicle before Walter had a chance to speak up. "Thank you, Walter. Bye, Walter." Walter took that as a firm response before driving home.

Nelly immediately moved to Kansas City, where she took classes as a stenographer and found lodging at a boarding house. Staying at the same boarding house was Paul Donnelly, a

Kansas City shoe company salesman. Paul was a man of average height, yet carried himself as if he were an imposing figure. He felt entitled to the finer things in life, though his pocketbook screamed otherwise. Unlike Walter, Paul was straight to the point. He knew exactly what he wanted. And it was Nelly.

They married near her seventeenth birthday and his twenty-third. There were many personality traits that Nelly admired in Paul. The most important one was giving her her freedom to pursue any area of interest. She enrolled in college, leaving many of Paul's nights open to interpretation. She soon discovered that she was the driven one in their union. Paul, on the other hand, pursued his own interests — those of an adulterous kind.

Nelly knew her husband stumbled a time or two. She blamed herself because of the long hours she kept working as a stenographer and pursuing her education simultaneously. On a rare evening while both were home, Nelly decided that it was the time to discuss having a family. Nelly lit Paul's pipe and sat down next to him.

"Nelly, my dear, you have a knack for plucking the thoughts right from my head."

"Paul, I would like to have a baby."

. . .

Paul quickly snapped out of his love-fog. "We haven't the room, the time, and you don't have the predisposition for motherhood. That is precisely why I married you."

Though an insulting comment, Nelly kept her cool. "I wasn't predisposed to marriage, yet here we are."

Paul stood. "If you must have a baby, I shall commit suicide."

There it was. Though an abnormal and devastating response, it rolled off Paul's tongue as if he had ordered poached eggs and rye toast for breakfast. For Paul found it easier to dismiss the idea of children than to confide in Nelly that he feared he could not trade in one type of love for another; that sometimes love does have limits. Paul reveled in his selfish ways, finding her questions intrusive.

Nelly was quite shocked by Paul's admission. She had always seen herself as a mother, either with or without Paul. She knew she had a lot to offer a child. She had made a mistake in marrying a man clearly at odds with her own wants and desires. Paul's threat of suicide was just to make a point, but the statement alone was cause for anxiety.

THE BEGINNING

*I*n the years that followed, Nelly returned to making form-fitting, frilly frocks for everyday wear for herself and her neighbors. It first started with two sewing machines in her spare room. Her neighbors would drop by to be fitted and place their orders. Most bought two or more dresses at a time, as one dollar was a reasonable sum for a custom dress. One neighbor in particular, Margaret Langly, became Nelly's most frequent customer. Margaret, a rather muscular woman of forty, had always had a difficult time finding clothes to fit her pearish frame and ample bosom. She relied on Nelly to keep her up-to-date with the latest trends.

"Dear Nelly, I would much prefer the Kimono-cut frock this time, though I've only seen them on slender women. What do you think?"

. . .

Nelly flipped through several tables of fabrics before landing on a light linen, black in color, and a white one for contrast. "I can provide a back panel in black to narrow your appearance. The style is quite adaptable. Shall I add the tuxedo collar in white?"

Overjoyed, Margaret grabbed Nelly by the shoulders and gave her a robust hug. "Such a talent. Have you ever pondered the idea of bringing samples to a department store?"

At first Nelly brushed off the comment, as she did personally not know of a single woman who was in business for herself. But the more she thought about it, the more it gained traction in her thoughts. Perhaps she was not meant to just be a wife and possible mother. Perhaps she had it in herself to be something more. Her fleeting thoughts of doubt were being pushed aside by visions of her own line. She rationalized that she could, indeed, be more than a woman in a spare room sewing. Why couldn't she stand toe-to-toe with her idol, Coco Chanel? Her favorite Coco quote of "A woman should be two things: classy and fabulous" was the reason she designed dresses for women in the first place. For Nell envisioned ordinary women looking "fabulous" cleaning around the home and taking care of children in one of her custom frocks.

By the time Paul arrived home, Nelly had several samples prepared, along with a business plan and a list of local stores that sold boxy, unattractive, everyday wear for women. Paul was many things, but allergic to money was not one of them. He wholeheartedly endorsed her endeavor.

The next week, Nelly secured an appointment with the store buyer at George C. Peck Dry Good Company, the largest department store in the area. She had on occasion, window-shopped to her heart's content at Peck's, never once visualizing her dresses on their displays.

"I'm here to see Mr. Adams," Nelly announced.

"Whom shall I say is waiting?"

"Mrs. Nelly Donnelly," she quickly corrected herself, "Mrs. Nelly Don."

The secretary picked up the phone and dialed. "Mrs. Nelly Don is here to see Mr. Adams."

Nelly was ushered into an office that could only be described as lavish. Mahogany wood-paneled walls; intricate furniture pieces with mother of pearl and alabaster inlays. The ceilings were tray, lined with copper. The centerpiece of the room was not an object, but a single window which rose unobstructed from floor to ceiling, stretching fifteen-feet in width and height, exposing the Kansas City skyline. Embroidered satin drapes flanked both ends.

. . .

"Have a seat, Mrs. Don. Can I get you something?"

Nelly, unaware of the business etiquette, answered in the negative. "I'm fine. Thank you for seeing me."

Though the average housebound woman would feel intimidated amongst such grandeur, Nelly felt oddly strengthened. Mr. Adams, confident in his Oxford bag trousers and double-breasted vest with a single-breasted jacket, lit a Lucky Strike and dove straight to the point. Nelly could tell he was not a charmer and probably rose up the corporate ladder on pure style and steam.

"Show me what you have," Adams stated.

Nelly walked over to an empty rack and hung up ten dresses in order of color, from light to dark. Mr. Adams immediately inspected them thoroughly: the seams, hems, lining. "How long to make each dress?"

Without hesitation, Nelly said, "Two days; same quality."

"Do you use patterns?" he asked.

. . .

Nelly responded, "I make my own, in over twenty sizes." After a few moments of silence, an unabashed Nelly, who was accustomed to going out on a limb, added, "Your current inventory offers many choices for the twenty percent of women who dine out or the women who scrub floors, but nothing in-between. My collection is for the other eighty-percent."

Mr. Adams couldn't help but slightly part his lips and curl both corners of his mouth in smile. "I'll take eighteen… " he paused dramatically, then added, "dozen. To start."

Nelly could not believe her ears. Inside she quivered, yet outside, she was solid. "With assistance, I can have them to you within twenty days. Shall we talk about supplying your other stores?"

~

Once home, Nelly waited for Paul to return from work. Without saying a word, she dove into his arms, kissing him incessantly. Paul had no idea what the special occasion was, but enjoyed the spontaneous moment.

Within a year, Nelly and Paul had the business out of their home and into a small factory. With sixty-five employees, they were doing better than okay. Nelly had secured additional contracts with multiple stores within Kansas City with a goal to put a Nelly Don dress into every department store across the United States. Her vision never wavered.

THE FACTORY

A massive brick and mortar building, standing six stories high, covered an entire city block. Twenty-first Street and Grand Avenue, the former Coca-Cola building, was now the home of The Nell Donnelly Garment Company. Inside the first two floors could be found the executive offices, while on floors three through six, the clothing factory was in full production. Rows upon rows of sewing machine operators, cutters, assistant designers, merchandisers, totaled just over one thousand.

Nelly walked the floor of her factory with wide, concise, energetic steps to inspect and cover as much territory as possible. Her routine was to make her way to the sixth floor by two p.m., where she would share lunch with key staff after personally sewing a new garment each day.

. . .

During one morning survey, she noticed a young woman wiping tears from her eyes before completing a seam with bright yellow binding. Nelly approached the young woman.

"Ellie, is it?"

"Ah, yes, ma'am."

"Ellie, I thought we agreed, no more tears over unworthy suitors."

"Yes, ma'am, we did."

Nelly picked up the dress, "My favorite color. Do you know what it is?"

"No, ma'am."

"Yellow. It's the brightest hue in the spectrum. It's illuminating, offers hope, inspires original thought. It can awaken optimism and confidence. That's what I want for you, Ellie."

Ellie sat up straight, pulling her shoulders back.

. . .

"Now remember, all garments must be color-fast, durable, and of the utmost quality. You're my gal, Ellie. You're in a unique position to let me know if what you're working with doesn't meet our quality standards. I'm counting on you."

Ellie responds with a sense of pride, "No worries, ma'am."

"Swell, Ellie."

Nelly checked her Cartouche wristwatch for the time and adjusted the black silk ribbon. Most ladies of her distinction transitioned to the Cartouche with bracelets or chains, as they considered the ribbon out of fashion. But that didn't concern Nelly. She kept the ribboned wristwatch as a reminder of where she was just a few short years earlier. It was important to her.

It was 2:30 on a Wednesday. She was running late. Wednesday mornings Paul released the Nanny and watched over David before returning to the factory to keep the books in order. The afternoons belonged to her. Sweet David; his age still measured in months; totaling three.

David was quite a surprise to the couple. Not planned for, to say the least. In fact, the opposite held true. Making love for Nelly and Paul happened infrequently, which suited both fine. The energy involved in running such a massive company had taken its toll on both of them. However, when their libidos aligned, they used the withdrawal method. Afterwards, Nelly would use a Lysol disinfectant douche. This routine kept them baby-free for several years. Yet it seems the stork had other plans.

Nelly, knowing how Paul felt about having children and mastering the art of concealment through garments, kept the pregnancy shrouded until she no longer could. She found it better to deliver distressful news to Paul on a full stomach. Nelly told Paul while dining out at their favorite restaurant, between the rack of lamb and dessert. Paul was a picky, yet hearty eater.

"Waiter."

The waiter approached the table with hands folded behind his back. "How may I be of service?"

"These rosemary potatoes are too ... rosemary-ish. I expected more garlic," Paul complained.

"Shall I bring you garlic-roasted potatoes instead, sir?"

"Did I say I wanted garlic potatoes? No, indeed. I want rosemary potatoes without so much rosemary. Is that too much to ask?"

. . .

"No, sir," the waiter responded.

The waiter attempted to pick up Paul's plate, but Paul flicked his hand away. "I'm still working on this. Bring it on a separate plate."

"Yes, sir." The waiter left for the kitchen.

"Paul, why do you insist on ordering the same rosemary potatoes, when in fact you have never eaten them?"

"I will, when they are prepared to my liking," Paul justified.

Nelly put her fork down. She was a bit apprehensive of telling Paul, with the case of the rosemary potatoes having left a bitter taste. "You seem a bit stronger in body and mind than when we first married."

Paul surgically removed the last bit of flesh off his rack of lamb and sniffed it as if it were a fine wine before devouring it.

"Put your utensils down, Paul." When she had Paul's full attention she added, "I'm expectant."

. . .

Paul seemed confused. "Expecting what?"

Nelly rephrased. "I'm in a family way."

His eyes slowly widened; a look of panic and agitation crossed Paul's face. He stood, turned around, and looked for the waiter. "Where are those potatoes?" After a momentary lapse, he took his seat. "I don't know how to respond, how to verbalize— What would you like me to say?"

Nelly shook her head. "What do you believe would be the customary response for a husband who finds his wife in such a state?"

Paul pondered the words, cupped his hand over hers, and uttered, "I so love you, Nelly, but what would you like to do about it?"

Nelly removed her hand from the table. "Absolutely nothing."

The rosemary potatoes arrived. The prideful waiter spouted, "Fresh-grilled red potatoes with only a hint of rosemary."

Paul stood, "Take it back." Paul turned to Nelly, "I'll have the car pulled around." Paul walked out after leaving money for the bill.

.   .   .

The waiter masked his resentment through a forced smile as he cleared the table. Nelly gathered her purse and composure and made her way to the ladies' room. A bathroom attendant ushered her toward an empty stall. Nelly managed, "Thank you" before retreating into the solitude of the water closet. She steadied herself up against the wall with both hands on opposite sides. She was used to being strong and secure, but Paul's reaction had obliterated both. She pulled a handkerchief from her purse, but it was not enough to wipe away her tears or muffle her cry.

The bathroom attendant kept her distance, yet wanted to lend support. "Ma'am, can I get you anything?"

Nelly regained her composure and opened the water closet door. "A fresh handkerchief, please."

The bathroom attendant handed two of them to Nelly. It wasn't the best start toward motherhood. In fact, Nelly spent more time in bed from the stress of it all than normal. But over the final five months, Paul settled into the idea of fatherhood. He was comfortable with being excluded from the birthing room and instead met with male colleagues on David's day of birth, handing out and smoking rare cigars to celebrate.

Unlike most women of the time, Nelly took only a handful of weeks to recover from giving birth. In fact, she was back walking the factory floor in no time.

~

Outside the factory, Nelly met with her chauffeur, George, a 23-year-old educated Negro who took pride in his work. George was the first of his family to go to college with hopes of becoming an engineer. But in the meantime, he chauffeured for Nelly. George polished the side mirror of the spectacle that was Nelly's 1926 Lincoln convertible. Though they were in the 1930s, Nelly refused to elevate her automobile to the latest model. Nelly was considerate of the times in which she lived. Though she had to present herself as successful in order to bring in more business, unnecessary flashiness was not her style. Yes, that automobile was just fine. It was also George's favorite. George tipped his Homburg hat and opened the door for Nelly.

"No flat cap today, huh, George?"

"Do you like it?"

"Most definitely."

Nelly climbed into the ample back seat. George shut the door behind her and wiped the fingerprints away. Then he climbed into the driver's seat.

"Home, ma'am?"

. . .

"Yes, George."

They pulled away from the sidewalk into light traffic.

THE RING

*C*oncerned, George asked, "Little David still have the sniffles?"

"The doctor indicated that his fever was low grade. We had feared pertussis."

"Oh no, ma'am."

"Please don't worry, George. All is on the upswing."

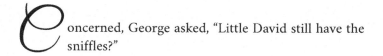

While Nelly was on her way home, Paul prepared for her arrival. Baby David slouched in his high chair and lost interest in his puffed wheat cereal. He swiped it off his tray and wailed.

. . .

PATRICE WILLIAMS MARKS

A woman, blond and busty, exited the bedroom and adjusted her skirt before addressing David's tantrum. She walked to the kitchen and grabbed a washcloth. She returned to wipe David's face, which was covered in dried mucus and cereal. "Aren't you the disagreeable one?" David seemed to have a bit of affection for her as he outstretched his arms in her direction. Right when she was about to release him from the highchair.

"Leave him be. I'll see to him," Paul pronounced.

She paused for a moment. "He is such a peach. I don't mind, really. Isn't that what you and Mrs. Donnelly hired me for?"

Paul opened the front door and gestured for her to make haste.

"If you insist."

The blonde reached for her overcoat and pocketbook; but not before giving David a goodbye kiss on the cheek. She glided past Paul, close enough to give him a final whiff of her perfume, which was aptly named Tabu; a sexy scent usually worn in evening. Paul inhaled, consuming the scent with an obvious appetite not soon to be doused. She exited as he shut the door after her.

· · ·

Paul made his way over to David and took him out of his highchair. He sat down with him on his lap, grateful that David's cold had been read its last rites. Paul was not one to make baby talk. No, in fact, Paul chose to speak to David as one adult would to another.

"Listen up, David."

David, oddly enough, ceased in the creation of spittle bubbles and listened intently.

"I may make mistakes. Some may even call me a bad man. But do you know what is most important in this life?"

David cocked his head to the side, the same way a puppy does when they try to understand words.

"Stature. Sin. Security. In that order. Absent any of those three, and you are doomed to a life of melancholy." Paul rose with David in his arms. "Time for your forty winks."

George made a left-hand turn and watched a car three vehicles behind, make the same turn, from his rearview mirror. That same car had matched their last two turns.

"You look distracted, George."

. . .

"Sorry, ma'am." He continued to drive, now only a handful of miles from their destination.

"Ready to make Judy an honest woman?" Nelly asked.

George smiled, "Judy and I are no longer courting."

"What a shame."

"It's fine, ma'am. A bit too sentimental. Teared up at the slightest discomfort, even in public places. Mary is the one for me."

"First Lana, then Judy, now Mary, all in the course of six months' time, George?"

George excitedly responded, "This is the one, ma'am. Got the rock in my pocket. Picked it up after only knowing her for ten days. Isn't that something?"

"Congratulations, George."

. . .

"Thank you ma'am. I figured I've wasted enough time, you know? Anxious to make it official. My pop's favorite quote is, "Life is short, God's way of encouraging a bit of focus.""

Nelly pondered those words before pulling out a hand-written letter from her purse. It was obvious the letter had been read and read again. Surprisingly, it had not disintegrated from her touch. But there it lay, between her two gloved hands. Plop. A tear landed on a page and threatened to discolor the ink. Nelly quickly wiped the tear away and stuffed the letter back inside her purse.

George pulled into Nelly's lengthy driveway that stretched an eighth of a mile to the main house. The estate sat comfortably on 2.3 acres. The brick mansion itself stood two stories tall with plantation pillars mirroring both sides of the entry. The lush trees, Amur Maples and Box Edders reached for the heavens at a stunning thirty-feet. The buffalo grass, a low-density turf, was now brown and dormant during the brisk Kansas September, a fact known to Nelly and weighing heavily in her decision to use it as sod. Although they were better than comfortable, using fewer natural resources to maintain their property was foremost in her mind. It was the Depression, and she was considerate of the lack of resources others faced.

The grounds were well-maintained by a small staff of two, educated in horticultural science. But today was Wednesday, and Wednesdays were their days off.

. . .

George stopped halfway up the driveway, as per Nelly's preference, so that she could enjoy the stroll the rest of the way up to the house. George put the car in park before he shut off the ignition. He reached for the door handle as a shadow crossed over his body. A Mauser C96 broom-handle pistol cocks, and "BAM ... BAM BAM." George slumped over the steering wheel.

Nelly jolted back and screamed, "George."

The masked hood pointed the still-smoking pistol at her temple, dead center. She raised her gloved hands, thereby knocking her purse to the floor of the convertible. He gestured for her to exit. She acquiesced.

Inside, Paul paused for a moment as he read the paper, unsure of what he may have heard. He decided to investigate. He neatly folded the newspaper and set it on a side table before he walked towards the window. But then the phone rang. Paul turned away from the window, just two strides away, and briskly made his way to the phone, where he picked it up.

Nelly hesitated for just a moment and placed one hand on George's shoulder before being yanked outside.

"Forget about that crumb. He's had his final kiss-off."

. . .

Nelly glanced at her home.

"It's alright, dollface. If you walk the line, we won't be filling little David and Paul with daylight. They're both in there, right, dollface?"

The masked hood shoved Nelly into the backseat of their car with a third accomplice behind the wheel. A burlap bag was violently pulled over her head. The stench of bovine was still embedded in its threads, a smell familiar to Nelly. He climbed in the back seat next to her with his pistol trained on her head.

The first hooded accomplice opened the driver-side door of Nelly's convertible and walked around to the passenger side. He climbed in, swung both feet up on the seat, leveraged against the dashboard and backrest to push George's body out of the vehicle. George slumped to the ground in a heap. His humble wedding ring for Mary tumbled onto the pavement. The hooded accomplice caught a glimpse of the shiny object out of the corner of his eye. He climbed out of the vehicle, picked up the ring, and inspected it using his second premolars before he pocketed it. He climbed into the driver's side, slammed that door, and started the engine. He backed out of the driveway and followed the lead car.

AN OPPORTUNITY

$\mathcal{L}$oud chimes filled Nelly's ears as her thoughts filled with panic. *Did I just witness George's execution? Where are they taking me? Will I ever see David again?* These thoughts, bundled up in shock, anger, and despair, swirled around her head and held.

Nelly sat on the floor of the back seat with her knees drawn close to her chest, hands tied together. For some reason, this position felt safe to Nelly. Well, as safe as she could possibly feel after being kidnapped. A whiff of an extrinsic scent lodged in her nostrils and caught her off guard. It was both lightly powdery and pungent at the same time. Her burlap sack was just loose enough for her to view the contents on the floor of the vehicle. A wrinkled sack with white flowers lay nearby. She recognized them as anemones.

The road was quite corrupted. Perhaps they had veered off the main thoroughfare. She focused her attention on the tenor of the world outside the car. Passing vehicles came and went with less frequency and no mandated stops. Nelly knew that if she was going to extricate herself from this catastrophic condition, she must act now.

Nelly surged upwards at such a speed and so unexpectedly, that the back of her head clocked the chin of the masked hood in the back seat, dazing him for a moment. She reached for the door handle, but it was locked. She felt for the locking mechanism along the window base and pulled it upwards, releasing the door. The driver, unable to aid in any way, shouted, "Knock the dame out, Jack. Clock the broad."

Jack, the masked hood, shook his head to regain his bearings. Nelly grabbed hold of the door handle, pulled down on it, and thereby jettisoned herself outside the speeding vehicle, with her face just inches from the rushing pavement. As she dangled, half inside, half outside, her brain pulsated and reacted to white light. Everything went blank for a moment before a flash of images zipped by: images of her sister Dot, Paul, David, Walter, her parents. Then a treasured memory seeped through.

The white light carried her back to an evening filled with clear skies with ten thousand stars. They were dancing, if she had to categorize it, but when two people slowly move from side to side, embracing without music, it could be labeled simply... existing. She was experiencing true bliss; a sense of calm that could not be described. He held her tight, whispered in her left ear a fraction of what he knew about the constellations. She discovered that once you stepped outside, you would have to wait a full thirty minutes before your eyes would register the multitude of stars, and that the naked eye could decipher over ten thousand stars, even with some being lost in a haze over the horizon. Every one of those ten thousand mattered to Nelly, as she wanted a lifetime under them with him.

Nelly was shocked back to the present as Jack grabbed the burlap bag around her head and used it to yank her back inside the vehicle before a passing vehicle approached. Nelly tumbled backwards and bounced off the back seat, back to the floor. Jack took the butt-end of his pistol and walloped the back of her head once. Nelly refused to stay down. He walloped her a second, and then a third time before Nelly collapsed unconscious. Jack was ready to smash her a fourth time when the driver spoke up.

"Jack, she's our butter and eggs."

Jack calmed down from his vengeful frenzy and leaned back in his seat. He cocked his pistol and pointed it at the driver. The driver eyed him from the rear view mirror. "Listen grease-ball, I'm the one facing the hot-squat. This is MY PARTY."

The driver raised one hand in a goodwill gesture, "Okay, okay."

. . .

The burlap bag over Nelly's head slowly became saturated with deep crimson blood. Wanting to make sure his latest capture was still alive, Jack lifted the bag off her face, and shook her by the chin. Nelly moaned. He lowered the bag back down.

THE ORPHAN

*T*he second hood, Thurmond, who drove Nelly's convertible, split from the lead car as planned. He was quite stimulated from driving such a fine machine. Although his orders were to camouflage the vehicle behind a billboard on an untraveled road, Thurmond rationalized that he would do just that, after he was good and ready. After all, Jack would never know.

Thurmond was comfortable with his patsy role and followed Jack's every command. It had been that way from the start. Thurmond was treated as an orphan, though everyone in town knew who his parents were. Hugh and Mabel were constants in the community for 19 years, known for caring more about appearances than proper decorum. They had three children. When the ill-favored child was diagnosed as being soft in the head, they felt no need to keep up pretenses. They simply dropped him off with a minister in the next town over when he was ten years old. Thurmond, feeling resentful, had no motivation to walk the straight and narrow.

Within a year, the minister had asked Thurmond to leave, which he did.

Thurmond met Jack that same day, watching him bump into a gentleman, and then make tracks with his wallet. As Jack counted his loot a few blocks away, Thurmond showed up. So did the coppers. Jack tossed the empty wallet at Thurmond, climbed over a wood-planked fence as the coppers turned the corner. Thurmond was questioned, and didn't say a word in his own defense, taking the rap for Jack. Jack watched the entire exchange from the other side of the fence. Once released after spending a week in the joint, Jack met up with Thurmond, deciding then and there that Thurmond would be his loyal patsy, while Thurmond decided then and there that Jack would be his older brother.

Thurmond flattened the gas pedal as the convertible sped up to an exceptional pace never experienced before by its driver. He was exhilarated by the power of this well-maintained, exceptional machine and took advantage of the open dirt road ahead. He flew over small humps in the road that gave him the feeling of flight. Faster and faster, dust bellowed behind him, leaving a cloudy trail of debris. At top speed, he swung the steering wheel sharply to the left. The car slewed across the road. A plume of dust and gravel sprayed up from the back wheels as they violently skidded around and released tire particles. Thurmond peered through the front windshield and realized he'd spun one hundred and eighty degrees. He hit the brake and jolted to a complete stop. He caught his breath. "What a tin can."

· · ·

Thurmond started up the vehicle again and headed towards the dilapidated billboard Jack pointed out to him earlier. He drove behind it and parked. He got out and rummaged for and found an old tarp. He used the tarp to cover the car before he walked back towards the dirt road. Still being a little soft in the head, he just realized that he no longer had wheels to meet back up with Jack. Figuring he was stuck in the middle of nowhere without transportation, he slapped his own mug with resentment. "Nothin' but a dumb egg, I am."

Thurmond saw no alternative but to start the long haul, as he put one foot in front of the other. As he walked in the center of the dead road, he tripped over a ragged pebble shaped like his deformed thumb. He giggled, delightfully picked it up, and compared it to his left thumb. He wiped it clean with his jacket and placed it in his pocket before he continued down the road.

After a few hours of huffing it, Thurmond spotted a farmer who drove an open-cab pickup that rattled down the road. He waved him down, and the farmer pulled over.

"Where you goin' son?"

Thurmond smiled, "Wherever you are, pops."

"Climb in the back."

. . .

Thurmond tipped his hat. As he walked along the side of the pickup, he ran his fingers along its edges, leaving a clean streak where mud used to be.

"I ain't got all day," the farmer pronounced.

Thurmond hopped in the back and joined the farmer's hound. He slouched next to the dog and stroked it as the pickup pulled away.

THE FARMHOUSE

*a*n abandoned farmhouse sat four acres back from any travelled road near Creamery Street, NE of Bonner Springs. With overgrown foliage, coarse woody debris, and fallen trees, the farmhouse itself had a sloped, disheveled porch with three beams that held up a dilapidated roof. Inside, a pile of discarded furniture sat in the parlor corner; paint was missing from the walls, showing peeling and chewed-away wallpaper from a bygone era. Strangely enough, the lead light and stained-glass windows in the sitting room alcove remained unadulterated, with their geometric pieces forming a wheat field design under the mid-afternoon rays. A blackened fireplace with fresh wood stacked inside was the focal point of the room. The driver, Earl, used a flint to start the fire. Jack commented, "Hurry up, bub, it's colder than a polar bears' nuts in here." Earl bunched up tinder in the center of the logs, removed a knife from his pocket, and struck it against the flint.

· · ·

Earl, a virile, college-educated, brawny, dapper-don, had an exceptional physique likened to Buster Crabbe's Tarzan. He finished his secondary education in record time, and was on his way to a promising career in finance— until President Herbert Hoover coined the word "Depression" to describe the rapid economic downturn. When the stock market took a slight dip, over three hundred traders threw themselves in front of locomotives. Earl's father was one of them.

Earl struck the flint once more ... success.

Nelly's clothing was in a heap next to the fireplace; her dress, gloves, coat, and shoes were piled high with no regard. Nelly sat, situated in a pressed-back oak Larkin chair with a wicker seat with ropes tied around her torso and with her hands pinned behind the back of the chair.

Nelly, a woman of good taste and proper decorum, was stripped of her dignity and laid barren in her undergarments before these distasteful hoods. Her complexion was usually white and waxen; her cheeks, a hint of pink; her hair crown slick, and the base of her hair voluminous. It was all exchanged for blood-soaked matting, bruised, and swollen cheeks. The burlap bag had been replaced with a blindfold, tight and restrictive. Hairs at the base of her neck were intertwined and were being pulled out from the follicles with the knot of the blindfold.

Jack approached Nelly, hovering over her. His breath smelled like a mixture of tobacco, disease and infection. "Nelly Don.

Has kinda a ring to it. Miss Nelly. Can I call you that? Miss Nelly, you done thrown us a curve ball, with hangin' out the car and all. What were you thinkin'?"

Nelly came to. She raised her head, realizing that she was bound. She struggled violently to free herself. Jack responded, "Don't flip your wig, Nell. You ain't goin' nowhere 'tils I says so."

Earl fingers Nell's dress, noticing the Nelly Don label in the nap of the dress. "Fine dress. A Nelly Don original. Classic workmanship."

Jack piped up, "What are you, a gunsel?"

Nelly spoke up. "The Donnelly Company can provide you with a generous benefaction —"

Jack cut her off, "A what?"

Nelly rephrased her words more carefully and concisely, "I apologize. You're holding me in exchange for —"

Jack responded, "Dough, pure and simple. You give us what we want and we'll deliver you back, lickety-split."

. . .

Nelly wanted to continue the strained conversation as this could be the only way to survive. "You know I have a son. Three months old. Do you have any children?"

Furious, Jack raised his hand, hauled off, and whacked her across the face with such a force that she was almost knocked off her chair. As her chair rocked back and forth from the blow, it came to an abrupt stop as Jack grabbed the back of the chair and steadied it. "Lesson one. I ask questions. You answer."

Nelly nodded, afraid to do anything but agree. Her face stung from the slap with red hot heat. Jack left the room.

In the car ride to the farmhouse, Nelly had worked on pure adrenaline. But now shock had set in with the realization of what was happening to her. Nelly's hands began to tremble, then her legs. Her pulse increased, then dropped. Her breath became slow and shallow; her pupils dilated. Nelly was confused, agitated and anxious all at the same time. Though dizzy and light-headed, Nelly remembered exactly the moment when George … She recalled the last conversation she had with George.

"This is the one, ma'am. Got the rock in my pocket. Picked it up after only knowing her for ten days. Ain't that something?"

"Congratulations, George."

. . .

"Thank you ma'am. I figured I've wasted enough time, you know? Anxious to make it official. My pops's favorite quote is, "Life is short, God's way of encouraging a bit of focus."

Nelly couldn't get George's words out of her head. She screamed at the top of her lungs. Her chest heaved up and down in rapid pulsation. She couldn't catch her breath. She panicked for a moment.

Jack stuck his head into the room, "No one can hear ya."

Nelly dropped her chin on her chest and sobbed … more tears than she had ever cried before. In between the tears, she ran through a laundry-list of regrets now that the life she knew had been turned sideways. *Why didn't I have more children? Why didn't we drive all the way up the driveway? We may have been able to escape if we had. Why did George have to pay the price for my success? Am I going to die today?*

Jack returned with a piece of paper and a pen. He masked himself once again. He untied Nelly's blindfold, yanked it off, and took several strands of hair with it. She opened her eyes to shards of debilitating light that flooded in, blinding her for a moment and burning her dilated pupils.

. . .

Jack loosened up a section of the rope and freed one of her hands. He shoved a piece of paper in front of her and unscrewed a pen from its barrel before handing it to her.

Earl grabbed his overcoat and headed outside where he ran into Thurmond. Thurmond had a smile plastered across his face for having the farmer drop him off two miles away, so as to not give away their location. He was proud for thinking things through and eager to brag to Jack. He raced inside.

Earl headed towards the barn and slid open the door to reveal rusted farm equipment, haystacks, and sacks of grain left behind by the vacated family. He heaved a grain sack onto a hook, removed his jacket, and rolled up his sleeves. He swung with a right hook, then left, uppercut, jab, jab, cross; each swing more vicious than the previous. He pounded away at the sack with intensity.

THE DISCOVERY

*D*avid had been asleep for an hour and forty minutes. That gave Paul precious moments alone. Paul reveled in the silence as he saw it as a commodity that couldn't be bought or traded. Growing up as an only child, Paul was expected to be seen and not heard. His adolescent ways were never tolerated.

Paul knew he was neither a planned nor a wanted child from his own mother. Gladys, a woman considered an old maid, married Paul's father, Mort, at the age of 31. It was not her beauty that captured Mort, as she was as plain as the day was long. It was her ability to keep house, prepare a fine meal, and know her place. To Mort, she was a woman of perfection.

However, this woman needed to be in control of some aspect of her existence. Paul became her figurative whipping post. A simple request to play outside was met with a tirade. Nevertheless, he pursued the elusive approval in hopes he could catch her at a weak moment.

"Ma'am, I cleaned my room and swept the walkway," an eight-year-old Paul declared.

"You will not receive accolades for simply doing your chores," his mother pronounced.

"I saw Ricky and Joe outside."

"They are dirty little cretins their mothers banish outside for sanity's sake."

"Yes, ma'am. I was wonderin' …"

His mother put down her needlework and shot him a look that quickly caused him to correct himself.

"I mean, I was wondering … it's still daylight … they're going to the park. I was wondering —"

"Wondering what, Paul? Wondering what?"

. . .

"Can I go, just this once, ma'am? Just for an hour? I promise—"

His mother took over the conversation. "You promise what, Paul? What do you have to barter with that I could possibly want?" She stood over him in such a way as to intimidate and frighten him. She wagged her finger ... "Do you know the pain and agony I went through giving birth to you? Because of you, I no longer have my girlish curves. No, I am saddled with darkened marks stretched across my belly, my thighs, my nether regions, all because of *you*. Doctors said that if I had a girl, my body would have adapted much easier to the change. But with boys, with their rough, careless, and selfish ways, they destroy and tear apart the female anatomy."

Paul took a few steps back towards his bedroom.

"Did I say you were dismissed?"

"No ma'am."

"How long do you think I have to live with this body you destroyed?"

Paul was unsure if it was a question she wanted a verbal response to.

. . .

"Forever. That's how long. Until I'm dead in the ground. That's how long. So until things change for me, they're not going to change for you."

Paul nodded his head in agreement; knowing that response was expected.

"Yes, ma'am."

Gladys sat back down and picked up her needlework.

"You may go."

Paul retreated to his bedroom as Gladys called out. "Leave the door open."

Paul left his bedroom door open as requested, but walked into his darkened closet. He shut the door behind him.

As the grown-up Paul checked in on David, he heard a knock at the front door. He quietly shut the bedroom door and walked downstairs towards the front of the house. Paul swung open the door and discovered no one there. He stepped outside and looked both ways; up and down the driveway. He noticed a mild dust cloud left from an exiting vehicle. He considered the entire incident odd and then turned to go back inside.

But at that very moment, he noticed a bouquet of white anemones on the porch swing. Curious, he walked over to the swing, picked up the flowers, and sniffed. A card fluttered to the ground. He bent down to pick it up. The note was made from newspaper headlines:

We have your Nelly Don.

At first Paul chuckled to himself— such tomfoolery. He carried the flowers inside, along with the note. He placed both on the table before he made a phone call.

"This is Paul. May I speak with Nell?"

"Nell is not here, Mr. Donnelly," the operator responded.

"When did she leave? Did she say she was heading straight —
"

"She was looking forward to seeing David, sir, with his cold and all. She was going straight home. That's what she told me, sir. Shall I check to see if her car is out front?"

"Yes, please do."

. . .

The phone went dead momentarily before the receptionist picked the receiver back up.

"It's gone, sir. Been told it's been over two hours ago."

A mild wave of panic creeped its way into Paul's psyche. He cleared his throat before he spoke up.

"I am sure there is a reasonable explanation. Good day."

Paul hung up the phone and picked up the newspaper-constructed note once more. He read and reread it. His heart began to palpitate. He paced back and forth before coming to a decision. He made another call, this time to their family attorney, James Taylor.

～

At that same moment, a newsboy raced into Taylor's office lobby; out of breath. Taylor's secretary blocked him from going any further.

"Pump your brakes, kid."

"I'm late, I have to see Mr. Taylor. Is that him?"

. . .

PATRICE WILLIAMS MARKS

"Who's asking?"

"I have this package, see? I have to give it to Mr. Taylor."

"I'm Mr. Taylor's Secretary. You can give it to me and I'll be sure he gets it."

"I was told to only give it to him," the newsboy proclaimed.

"By whom?" asked the secretary.

"He didn't give me his birth certificate, sister."

He tried to push his way past her, but she was not having any of it. She pulled out a dollar bill from her pocket and waved it in front of him.

"Let's say you gave it to him. Just between you and me, right?"

The newsboy shrugged, took the dollar, and handed the package over to the secretary, and then took off as quickly as he arrived. The secretary carried the package to her desk and reached for a pair of scissors. She cut the twine from the package and unfolded the butcher paper. She saw a "Nelly Don" label stitched inside the collar of a dress. She lifted the garment from the package to reveal a garment in a ravaged state, along with blood on the outside collar and down the front of the dress. Some of it was still moist. She dropped the dress on her desk in a heap when she spotted the note. She recognized the handwriting as Nelly's.

She called out in a panicked state, "Mr. Taylor."

THE SCOTCH

*T*he office phone rang, yet no one answered. It continued to throb and pulsate with annoying, high-pitched tones.

A robust man of sixty, James Taylor, Esquire, was quite occupied with the stacks of folders on his desk. And when he was occupied, his mind blocked out all other distractions.

He shifted through one pile, then the other, unable to put his finger on the court document he sought. He removed his spectacles and rubbed the smudges off the lens with a soft cloth before placing them back on. He used his index finger to adjust their position.

"Ms. Brand. Come here at once after you answer that phone." He paused, fully expecting the ringing to stop. It continued.

. . .

"Ms. Brand?"

Ms. Brand appeared in the doorway, holding the butcher paper and dress in one hand and the note in the other.

"Ms. Brand. You look a fright. What is it?"

"Mr. Taylor…"

Taylor gestured for her to come forward, which she did. She gently placed the items on his desk as if they could explode at any moment. "What is this?"

Taylor inspected the dress and the butcher paper. His demeanor changed from frustration to confusion. Ms. Brand handed him the handwritten note from Nelly. He read it out loud:

> *I attest that I am Nell Donnelly.
> I have been taken hostage.
> George has been killed. They
> want $75,000 or I'll be blinded
> and killed. They will be in touch.
> Nell*

Taylor picked up the ringing phone. It was Paul. Taylor snapped his fingers, gestured for Ms. Brand to get him a pen and paper, lickety-split. She did so immediately. Taylor listened intently to Paul as he wrote down extensive notes.

. . .

Taylor spoke in both a calming and in-control manner.

"Paul— Paul, listen to me. Paul. Paul, have you called the police? Are you sitting down, Paul? We just received... Paul, what was Nelly wearing today, can you describe it?"

By the response he received, Taylor simply confirmed what he already knew. "Paul, we have Nelly's dress... yes, here. It was delivered. No, no, Nelly should still be alive, Paul. Ransom is what they want. She has to be kept alive. They want seventy-five thousand. Yes, I know you want to pay it straight away. But I ask of you dear friend, to take one step backwards, to compose yourself. We can't make any mistakes. You've called the police. Now I've got a call to make. What's that? White flowers? Can you describe them?"

Taylor exchanged knowing glares with Ms. Brand. After a few more comforting words, Taylor hung up the phone. Taylor slammed his fist on top of his desk with as much brute force as a sledgehammer levies against a carnival game.

"Get me Reed."

"Yes, sir," the secretary responded.

～

Successions of police cars arrived outside the Donnelly residence. They stopped halfway up the driveway once they spotted George's body. Police Chief Harrison, a man with a strong constitution and a weak jaw line, gestured for half the cars to go up to the house and the other half to stay with him. Known for having a lousy track record for convictions and running slapdash through cases, most prominent citizens saw fit to go over his head with all legal concerns. Unfortunately, his superior had recently passed on, leaving a vacancy that Harrison intended to fill. This case would be his opportunity to turn a ragged-edged corner and rebuild his reputation. He climbed out of the vehicle, chewed on his unlit tobacco pipe, which was a habit strictly for show.

Harrison barked, "Sanders, I want you to cordon off this area twenty feet by twenty. Bailey, head back down the driveway and use your car to block the driveway. The shit is about to hit the fan, and the longer we can keep the badgers at bay, the better."

"Yes, Captain."

"Will do, Captain."

Sanders and Bailey followed his orders. Harrison gestured for another officer to follow him to George's body. He bent down and eyeballed the corpse.

"Nasty business," Harrison commented.

. . .

Harrison gently turned George over from his belly to his back, revealing a large wound where blood gushed out.

"I'd say the mug was less than five feet away, the caliber, thirty-eight or thirty-two," Harrison surmised.

"How's that, Captain?"

"The pattern around the entrance wound, that's how," Harrison shared.

Harrison pulled open George's shirt and exposed the wound. It showed an abrasion ring and a slight imprint of the weapon's barrel. The police photographer arrives.

Harrison rose to greet him, "He's all yours."

The photographer held a high-speed camera with flash bulb illumination and positioned himself for the first round of shots. The flash bulb burned and popped. The photographer reached into his pocket to replace it.

"Do you mind, Captain?"

"Go ahead," Harrison approved.

. . .

The photographer rolled George back over, face down, to stage his second set of photos.

Harrison called Bailey over.

"Get the meat wagon. Wait with—"

Harrison bent back down, reached in George's pockets, and pulled out his wallet before standing back up.

"—George Blair. Nobody else comes within ten and ten."

"Yes, Captain."

~

Harrison made his way towards the Donnelly home. He admired the grounds before he knocked on the front door. An officer swung the door open.

"Where is Mr. Donnelly?" Harrison asked.

"In the kitchen." The officer gestured in that direction.

Harrison made note of the view of the driveway and expansive acreage from the front window before he headed to the kitchen. There he found Paul at the kitchen table with a tall glass of scotch and a near-empty bottle. He looked like Hell.

"Mr. Donnelly, I'm —"

"I know who you are, Captain Harrison. Just our misfortune."

Harrison ignored the snipe and pulled out a chair from the table.

"May I?"

Paul ignored the request and took a measured sip of scotch, studying it intently. Harrison grabbed a seat across from him.

"That's Glenlivet, twelve year-old single-malt scotch isn't it?"

Paul looked at him quizzically.

"I have to say that it is, in general, uninspiring, and the aftertaste is quite acidic. Don't you agree?"

. . .

Paul responded, "If that was your attempt to convince me of your knowledge on such cases... you failed."

Paul swished the remainder of his scotch from cheek to cheek before swallowing it in one gulp. With a tight grip on the empty glass, he slammed it down on the table, sending shards in every direction.

THE INVESTIGATION

*H*arrison, cool as a cucumber, searched the room for a broom and dustpan. He found one behind a closed door to the cupboard. He removed his jacket and rolled up his sleeves before sweeping up the broken glass. He left the glass pieces in the dust pan before returning to the table.

"What is Mrs. Donnelly like?" Harrison asked.

Paul was a bit put off, "Excuse, me?"

"I've done my homework. Mrs. Donnelly is quite the woman. You two started the Donnelly Garment Company less than seven years ago, and in that time you've grown to become one of the largest employers in this state. You employ over one thousand people, mostly women. You see to their health needs, higher education, and childcare. Your dresses are the number one seller in thirty-eight states and ten countries. All this I know. What I don't know is, what is Mrs. Donnelly like?"

Paul, surprised by Harrison's knowledge, asked a follow-up question.

"At home or at work?"

Harrison scooted his chair closer to Paul for a more intimate conversation.

"Is she a patient woman? Will she follow orders? The hoodlums that have Nelly —"

"You know who they are?" Paul shouted.

"We have an idea. Those torpedoes are out to bleed you. That's it. If Mrs. Donnelly —"

"Nelly. She goes by Nelly," Paul said, his breathing ragged and his head in one hand.

Harrison responded, "Excuse me, Nelly. If Nelly is as smart as I think she is, she'll survive this. She will return home to you and your son. But deviating from any demands will put her in further danger."

Paul rose. "Nelly is the smartest woman I know. Can you promise me that if Nelly does exactly as they say, and we give them what they want, that she will be returned alive and unharmed? Can you guarantee that?"

Harrison scooted his chair back and stood as well. "What I can promise you is that you and your family are our top priority. By the time we're through, no rock will be left unturned, nor any dark place that these pieces of filth can hide, that we haven't unearthed. That I can guarantee you."

Harrison extended his hand to Paul, who paused a moment before shaking it.

"What do I do? Tell me." Paul asked with a vulnerable tone.

Inside Taylor's law office lobby, two beat cops took away the clothing and note left by the newsboy as evidence. His secretary walked them to the door. Taylor was in his private office on the phone with Senator Reed.

"Senator Reed, I have some quite disturbing news," Taylor expressed.

. . .

"Hurry up, man, I'm due back in chambers," Senator Reed said briskly.

Taylor took a deep breath before he slowly exhaled. "Young Brook Hart."

Senator Reed recollected, "Yes, such a calamitous turn of events. You know, James, I blame myself."

Taylor was surprised by the proclamation, "Reed, you moved Heaven and Earth. There was no way—"

Reed jumped in. "I gave my word to his family. I'm not a man who takes such oaths without considering all that is to be considered. Weighing the proposed outcome against evidence, then rendering a decision based on palpability."

"You may have another opportunity, Reed. What is it that they say about redemption? That misfortune breeds redemption?" Taylor added.

This statement piqued Reed's interest. He sat up straight in his leather, high-backed chair.

Taylor continued, "Remember the white anemones sent to the Harts?"

. . .

Reed responded, "Of course."

"They've been sent to another one of your constituents. This time a woman has been abducted. You may remember the family: Paul and Nell Donnelly. They're also my clients. As you may recall, she's the famous dress designer."

Reed didn't let him finish his sentence. "Yes, yes, I know who she is." He tightened his grip on the phone receiver.

"The police say it's the same gang."

Reed jumped to his feet. "When did this happen?"

"Earlier today. Paul is speaking with the police right now. George, her chauffeur, was executed during the abduction. Horrible waste of a good man."

There was silence on the other end of the phone. Taylor spoke up. "Reed? Reed, are you there?"

After another moment of stillness, Reed spoke up. "What do they say about Mrs. Donnelly?"

"They have her. All indications say that she is still alive."

. . .

Reed gathered up the paperwork on his desk into a pile before shoving it into a worn leather satchel.

"I'm on my way."

Reed hung up the phone and called his secretary in. He told her to cancel all meetings and that he was on his way back to Kansas City from the State Capitol on a matter of the utmost urgency. She nodded in agreement before closing his office door behind her.

This abduction had knocked the wind out of Reed. He remembered Mrs. Nell Donnelly very well. In fact, their first meeting was at a private fundraiser held by Reed's wife, Barbara Ann, just a little over a year ago.

Fundraisers were never Reed's strong suit; in fact he would sooner give up all things related to capital campaigns, if he could remain in office without them. His wife, Barbara Ann, thrived in such circumstances; handling all of his funding duties and responsibilities with exuberance. Her delicate demeanor won over even the stingiest of opponents.

It was April 3, and it was a gathering of Kansas City's elite. Barbara Ann saw to it that politicians, business owners, and old-money families were represented. Her goal was to raise twenty-thousand for this campaign. She exceeded her goal by eight thousand.

. . .

Nell and Paul Donnelly arrived on time, which meant they were the first ones there. Barbara Ann made sure they had drinks in their hands before the front door shut. Reed recalled Paul having an added interest in Barbara Ann's womanly curves. Paul was not the first man to notice; nor would he be the last. Reed learned years ago not to step in such situations, as Barbara Ann resented it. In fact, she used it to her advantage when getting them to sign a fat check for whatever cause she was pushing at the time.

Barbara Ann was in her element. She relished sharing the story of how she and James met to every attendee who would give her an ear. She discovered that, by exposing such an intimate story, she gained their trust and thereby their wallet.

Barbara Ann never deviated from the story. Her car had a flat tire during the busiest time of day. Other vehicles were glee-fully passing her by without a thought. So there she stood, helpless on the side of the road. She decided to have a good laugh about her circumstance, as that was all she could do. Reed drove past and saw this woman laughing to herself, so he pulled over and asked her why she was laughing. Barbara Ann said she had two choices; she could be dismayed or see the humor in the situation. She chose to see the humor. Reed took her to the nearest repair shop where they sent someone out to tow the vehicle back in. During those few hours of waiting on the car, they fell in love. Five weeks later, they were married.

. . .

It made for such a refreshing conversation... despite the fact that it was entirely fabricated. Reed and Barbara Ann were introduced though their inner circle, and it was a business decision to marry, not love. But Barbara Ann rationalized that this story would be far more entertaining.

Nell Donnelly, a woman the opposite of Barbara Ann, carried herself in such a way as to command attention purely by her presence alone. Used to being the only woman in the boardroom, Nell relied on pragmatism, rather than feminine wiles, to make it in her male-driven industry.

Reed raised his voice from across the room.

"May I refresh your drink?"

Nelly looked over her shoulder before turning towards him. She raised her full glass.

"Where shall I put it? Shall I carry two glasses?"

Reed cocked his head to the side as her response was quite unexpected. Several other invited guests arrived, filling up the room with polite conversation and cigar vapor.

Barbara Ann, knowing that Nelly was the powerful figure behind the Donnelly Garment Company, whispered in

Reed's ear, "Nelly Don, owner of the Donnelly Garment Company. Her husband Paul is President, but everyone knows who holds the purse strings. She's good for five thousand. Go make conversation, and for God's sake, stay away from your political yarns. We don't want to bore her to death."

Reed whispered back, "Darling, your slip is showing."

Embarrassed, Barbara Ann backed out of the room and made her way to the servants' quarters to adjust her garment.

Reed moved towards Nelly, weaving though a cluster of servers and Kansas City's elite. He patted backs, greeting them all before introducing himself to Nelly.

"Please allow me to introduce myself, I'm—"

Nelly quipped, "Senator James Reed. Yes, I know. Beautiful home. Thank you for the invitation."

"We are pleased that you and Paul were able to join us this time."

Nelly smiled, "Barbara Ann would not accept 'perhaps' as an RSVP."

. . .

Reed smiled, "She would be more than happy to give you a guided tour. She's quite over-the-moon about a new porcelain china pattern. Though I believe it's actually from England. You'll have to ask her for the specifics."

"May I ask you a question, Senator Reed?"

"By all means," he said.

"Though you are comfortably at odds with the Hoover administration, I was surprised that you agreed with their tactics to gain the President popularity points by deporting five hundred thousand foreign-borns as a remedy for the depression. Families have been rounded up and plucked from their lives to be unceremoniously dumped in Mexico; many of them natives of other countries. How exactly is that helping our economy?"

Reed, shocked by her bold statement, responded. "Mrs. Donnelly—"

"Let's not stand on pretense. Please call me Nelly."

"Nelly, I had no idea you followed matters of state."

Paul glanced over at the impending storm that was Nelly and politics. He made no effort to interfere. He simply sought out

Barbara Ann, who had returned. Their conversation encompassed less treacherous waters; that is, the current weather conditions.

Nelly sipped from her champagne glass, "I do more than just follow, Senator."

Quite perturbed, Reed responded. "Shall we change the subject, as no spare room exists past your gums for a second foot?"

"I apologize if answering to your constituents leaves you in an uncomfortable state, Senator."

Reed's voice raised along with his blood pressure. He was now on the attack as if on the Senate floor. Other guests picked up on the lively conversation, with most expressing their disapproval of Nelly though whispers and gradual distance.

"My dear Mrs. Donnelly, you spout opinions without a thorough understanding of the democratic process."

"On that note, you are misinformed, Senator," Nelly contended.

. . .

Reed realized this woman would not be dismissed so easily.

"No man is an island. In order to get this country out of its devastating and self-imposed circumstances, decisions have been bartered. Some are not so popular. Swift, critical changes that will bring this country from the brink were released from the quagmire that is Congress. And do you know why, Mrs. Donnelly? Because of the deportation of non-citizens."

Barbara Ann left Paul's side and emerged from the crowd. She gently placed her hand on Reed's shoulder. It had no effect.

Nelly spoke, "I am not a naive woman, Senator Reed. I understand that only light can part darkness. But please understand, that the bartering between an elite group of men, made on behalf of the masses, must stand up to scrutiny. Isn't that what our democratic process ensures?"

Senator Reed paused a moment before answering.

"We are entrusted by the American people, Mrs. Donnelly. And I can assure you we carry that responsibility on our backs, every minute of every second of every day."

Senator Reed downed the rest of his champagne.

. . .

"Good day, Mrs. Donnelly."

Reed crossed over to a group of gentleman and joined in their conversation, a much more jovial one than the last.

FAILURE

*T*hat first introduction to Nelly left an unfavorable impression on Reed. He decided, then and there, that if he never crossed paths with this one-woman artillery launcher again, it would be too soon.

Unfortunately, their paths did cross again, this time at the Kansas Statehouse in Topeka.

The Donnelly Garment Company had put in a low and fair bid to make women's military uniforms. With the occupation of Nicaragua and Haiti, the United States relied heavily on a female workforce and female military personnel on United States soil.

Nelly designed uniforms that were flattering, even though they stuck to the strict military dress code standards. Paul brought the idea to Nelly and pitched it as a way to further raise their bottom line. He had done extensive research on their costs in comparison to what they could charge the government. Nelly agreed wholeheartedly to the proposal, with the exception of the actual bid amount. She refused to be a war profiteer. She cut the bid amount by one-third as she felt fifteen-percent over costs was plenty.

They were awarded the contract. Nelly personally went to the State Capitol to sign the contracts. With notarized documents in hand, Nelly left the state procurement office and ran straight into Reed in the hallway. She politely greeted him.

"Hello Senator Reed. Nice to see you again," she said before continuing down the corridor.

Reed responded, "Mrs. Donnelly. Congratulations."

Nelly paused. "Why, thank you."

Reed continued, "You were quite the center of attention over these past few months."

"Excuse me?"

"Yes, who is this Donnelly Garment Company, and how can they produce acceptable garments for two-hundred percent lower than the next bidder? They must have an inferior product, or they are not to be trusted, my colleagues assured the procurement director."

Nelly smiled. "And what say you, Senator Reed?"

"Not a thing, there was no need. Every secretary in every office on the hill owns at least one of your garments. They pronounced that the quality and reputation of the company speaks for itself. There you have it. An army of muliebrity at your service."

Nelly changed the subject to something she had meant to impart to the Reeds for several months, but she had never had time to follow through.

"You must convey to Barbara Ann my apologies for the disruption. At times I allow my convictions to take center stage when they should be as an understudy, sidelined until called upon."

Reed shook his head, "Neither of us bear you any malice, Nelly. In fact Barbara Ann has already added the Donnellys to her social directory. She says prospective fireworks are good for the bottom line."

"I agree. Good day, Senator Reed," echoing his last words to her from the party. Reed recognized this and was a bit amused. Nelly headed towards the exit at the end of the hallway.

~

Those memories stood out in Reed's mind, along with the conversation he had with Alex Hart, the father of young Brook, who had been beaten, thrown off a bridge, and then shot to death. Two days after Brook's abduction, Reed went to the Hart home and met with Alex to reassure the family that they would get their son back.

There were torrential rains that November 17th, keeping most decent folks near the fire. The Harts had been up for forty-eight straight hours, waiting on positive word regarding their Brook. They had been assured and reassured by Captain Harrison that Brook would more than likely be returned unharmed. He was one of many high-profile kidnappings, including that of William Hamm, an heir of a beer-producing family. Hamm was freed after a ten thousand dollar ransom was paid. This was good news and much-needed hope for the Harts.

But those were desperate times. The streets were filled with idle men, frantic men unable to provide even the basic necessities for their starving families. So they resorted to the abduction of the "haves."

Reed, a long time friend of the Harts, stepped in to make sure mistakes were not made. He sat down with the family in Alex Hart's study. Photos of all their children lined the walls. Brook's image was not a photograph, but a portrait. It hung behind Alex's desk in a place of prominence.

. . .

Reed shared with the Harts what he had learned from the FBI; that Brook was taken in a parking garage. According to an eyewitness, the men waited for Brook at the exit gate. Once Brook slowed down, they jumped inside the car, plunged a gun into his side and ordered him to drive. They were last seen on Market Street.

The Harts consumed every detail, charting out his known whereabouts and actions by the half-hour, on a roll of butcher paper spread out across a desk. They seemed to derive comfort from charting the specifics of his case.

Reed had placed a solid hand on Alex Hart's back and told him that half of Kansas was out looking for Brook, and that their agony would be short-lived. Reed could only sympathize with the Harts, as he had not raised any children of his own, a fact never brought up by Alex.

That same evening, Alex showed Reed the white anemones that were left on their front steps trumpeting Brook's abduction. Neither the police nor the FBI could come up with a rational explanation why those particular flowers were used or had been chosen.

Reed stayed in contact with the Harts in the three weeks that followed without a break in the case. The ransom had been paid, but Brook had not been released. This was not the normal protocol. With every passing day, Reed grew to accept the fact that Brook would never return. He kept those thoughts to himself, still offering hope to the family whenever a new bit of information was obtained.

Eventually, two duck hunters had come across a small bundle floating in the water. They rowed towards it, a discovered it was a corpse. They lifted the body on board, rowed back to shore, and called the coroner's office and the police. The body had been ravaged by eels and crabs. The face and hair had been eaten away, and its hands and feet were missing. The teeth were too damaged or missing to be of use to the police or FBI. Most of the abdomen was gone as well, making it extremely difficult to make an identification. A friend of the Harts went to analyze the clothing worn by the corpse. He spotted a gold clasp with Brooks initials inserted in the shirt's collar.

Reed was not a man to give way to distress, yet he did, once he heard Alex Hart proclaim at a press conference, "My boy is gone."

Reed grabbed his leather satchel, coat, and hat and exited his office in the State Capitol. He was on his way back to Kansas City to see about Nelly Don.

THE OUTHOUSE

*E*arl untied Nelly from the chair and stood her up. She was unsteady on her feet. Earl leaned her against him as he put his arm around her waist and walked her to the front door. He swung the door open with his free hand. Nelly, who was still blindfolded with her hands tied, needed precise directions to continue.

"There are three steps coming," Earl said.

"Where are we going?" Nelly asked.

Nelly used her right foot to feel for the first step, found it, then stepped down, once, twice, a third step until both feet were on the ground. Nelly pulled herself away from Earl and slumped to the ground. She blindly grabbed handfuls of earth and let them flow back to the ground in-between her fingers at a reluctant pace.

. . .

Earl grabbed hold of her arm and pulled her back up on her feet. He led her to the outhouse. He placed her hands on the door.

"You have five minutes."

Nelly searched for the handle with her fingers before locating it. She pushed open the door and let herself in. The door swung shut behind her and created a loud *boom*.

Earl lit a coffin stick and took a few puffs while he waited.

Inside, Nelly pulled down her undergarments and took a seat. She removed the blindfold. It took several moments for her pupils to adjust. She studied all four walls of this new prison and looked for an escape. There were two moon-shaped cutouts on opposite sides for ventilation. She contemplated screaming once again, but quickly ruled that out as she couldn't hear any nearby street traffic or farm life. No one would hear her. The only purpose it would serve would be to infuriate her captors.

No, there was but one possible way to escape. For no woman of Nelly's stature would even contemplate such an escape. They would rather succumb at the hands of their kidnappers than crawl through ordure. Yet Nelly thought about every avenue, no matter how distasteful.

Little Nell, having been raised on a farm, searched for unusual ways to entertain herself and her siblings. Horse-shoes, jacks, and marbles became tiresome to a child with such creative ways as Nelly. She thrived on taking and winning bets, never losing a one. Not even the surefire loser that Dot once concocted.

"I'll bet you can't find a way out of that stinky 'ole outhouse without using the door." Dot beamed, knowing she had finally put one over on Nell.

"How much you wanna bet, Dot?"

Dot, normally with an entire list of demands on the tip of her tongue, thought this one through for several moments before coming up with a whopper.

"'If you can't find a way out, you tend to the hogs for a month, milk that crazy heifer for two weeks, and carry my school books to and fro."

Nelly grinned before rattling off her own demands. "And if I win, you have to take me on all your dates for a month. No more petting parties."

Dot, shocked, replied, "Nell."

. . .

"You pay for my movie fare and popcorn. Afterwards, I want an all-the-way with extra whip cream and a cherry on top. Deal?"

Dot hesitated for a moment. Have this one tailing her for a month? But she surmised that no way Nell could pull this one off.

"Agreed."

Nell folded up the sleeves on her dress and removed her shoes. Dot plopped herself on the ground, surrounded by her other siblings.

Nell approached the outhouse as if sneaking up on it would relay hidden secrets to her. She plugged her nose by pinching her nostrils shut and held her breath before stepping inside. The door slammed behind her with a *bang*. She immediately scooped up some powdered lye with a wooden ladle and poured it over the contents of the pit. The smell subsided. She was able to breathe.

Nell pounded on all sides of the outhouse, determined to find a loose board that she could pry up and exit from. Outside, Dot rolled with laughter. Her other siblings joined in the hilarity.

. . .

Nell would not give up, even after thirty minutes of searching. Determined to win, Nell threw her weight onto the sides of the outhouse and created a slight rocking motion. This was all the encouragement she needed. She bounced from one side to the other. There was further motion, yet still not quite enough.

Nell rested a bit before trying the same strategy on the front and back walls this time. She threw her weight against the front door, then the back wall and created a seesaw effect. Outside, Dot's mouth fell agape. Inside, Nell gave one final push against the back wall. Success. The outhouse fell backwards off its foundation. However, the momentum of the rocking unexpectedly propelled Nell backwards, casting her into the now-exposed pit. She landed with such a thud that its contents flew out on all sides. Dot was beside herself in hysterics. Sure Nell had won, but it was so worth it.

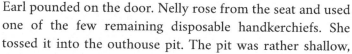

Earl pounded on the door. Nelly rose from the seat and used one of the few remaining disposable handkerchiefs. She tossed it into the outhouse pit. The pit was rather shallow, measuring about three-feet deep and four-feet across, she estimated.

Nelly's eyes shot towards the ceiling, where she observed cracks and rotting wood planks rattling from a sudden wind gust. She stood up on the seat and steadied herself. She strained to acquire a long sliver of wood.

· · ·

Outside, Earl shouted, "You almost through, sister?"

Nelly called out, "Almost."

Nelly used her fingernails to dislodge the sliver of wood. Although only a couple inches in diameter and maybe four-inches long, it would do. Nelly stepped off the seat. She shoved the wood sliver down the back of her undergarment. She had no idea of when she would use it, but she would. Nell thought to herself, *Violence begets violence. I will kill if I have to, to return to my family.*

Without warning, the outhouse door swung open, and Jack stood right in front of her. He looked exactly like what she had pictured. He wore a wrinkled three-piece suit, short-cropped haircut with an off-center part, and was unshaven.

Jack was caught off-guard when their eyes met. He shouted to Earl, "You louse. Where's the blindfold?" Panicked, Nell reached for the blindfold and handed it to Jack.

"Turn around," Jack demanded.

Nell did as instructed. Jack retied the blindfold then spun her around. He grabbed her arm and pulled her from the outhouse. The jerky motion dislodged the wood sliver from Nelly's undergarment and it slipped to the ground.

. . .

Jack didn't notice. He stepped right over it and dragged Nelly back to the house. Earl followed.

THE LINEUP

*T*he police precinct sat on the corner of Lakewood and Church. It had been here for as long as the town had been in existence. This aesthetically pleasing building respected the fabric of the neighborhood by echoing its design influences with a brick exterior, columnar entry-way, and distinctive keystones.

The first floor was surprisingly tame with activity, as it was used, more or less, as a pass-through to all key departments.

Up on the second floor, Harrison's office was located in the far corner, away from the beehive of activity. He liked it this way, as he found it hard to think otherwise. He was also better able to keep certain information from spreading to the precinct cops who were in the pocket of Lazia.

· · ·

John Lazia, a powerful Kansas City gangster, had virtual control over the city and the precinct through intimidation, bribery, and assignations. Lazia even induced the hiring of known criminals as policemen. These operatives of his, when called upon, acted as their own independent police force.

Harrison had zero control over pocketed cops, yet he did exercise control over those in the precinct who still remained on the straight and narrow. The difficulty arose for Harrison when trying to distinguish between the two. There were two young beat cops that he kept on a short leash, watched over their activities closely, and had come to trust. Their names were Bailey and Sanders.

Sanders rapped his knuckles on Harrison's door, which was solid mahogany with a glass window at the top. Harrison gestured for him to come in.

"They're ready for you, Captain."

Harrison responded, "How many?"

Sanders answered, "Seven."

Harrison placed a bottle in his pocket and came out from behind his desk.

. . .

"And, Captain?"

"Yes?"

"He's arrived, waiting with the rest."

Harrison glided through the precinct on a mission. Sanders followed behind, taking two steps for every one of Harrison's. Harrison walked into a room with several folding chairs. However, no one was sitting. The room was dim and obscured the faces of these men. In front, there was a stage with its main attraction, a lineup. Harrison waved the seven suspects in. Bailey grabbed hold of the arm of the first suspect and pulled him towards the stage. These men knew the drill. One after another stepped up onto the platform. Bailey called out, "Go to the end, mac." The suspect tipped his hat and obliged. The other six suspects stood alongside the first. They were a ragged group of misfits, except for number two, who, despite his low-class threads, stood tall and proud. Several flood lamps flashed on simultaneously, temporarily blinding the suspects.

"Clear away your lids," Bailey mandated. The suspects removed their hats. Number two was the last one to do so. Harrison commanded the room. "Number one, please step forward." The suspect obeyed.

"State your name for the record."

. . .

"Benny the Boy, Captain."

Harrison continued, "Benny the Boy Johnson, when's the last time you had some hooch?"

Benny rubbed his unshaven jaw, "Been twelve and a half hours."

Harrison pulled out a bottle of whiskey from his pocket and tossed it to Benny. Benny dropped his hat to catch the bottle. He immediately unscrewed the top and took a swig.

"We know you have nothing to do with Nelly Don's kidnapping."

"Who?" Benny the Boy asked.

The only man who was sitting in the room nervously clutched his coat pocket. He leaned forward and made sure not to miss a single word or confession.

"Don't play dumb with me, Benny. We know that we know you have an ear to the pavement. If someone kites a loaf of bread, you fink to the baker."

. . .

PATRICE WILLIAMS MARKS

The rest of the men in the shadows howled and snorted with laughter, except for the man who sat.

Benny took another swig, "That rich broad? I don't know nothin'. I'm no canary."

Bailey walked up to Benny and snatched the bottle away. The suspect next to Benny whispered to him, "That's right, Benny Boy."

Harrison jumped up on stage and stood right in front of suspect number two. Sully, a two-bit hood with scuffed shoes and an over-sized jacket, took it all in stride. It was apparent that he was no virgin when it came to lineups.

"And you're Sully, one of Lazia's men."

Sully smirked without confirming or denying.

"You're all wet, Sully. Tell me, how much did Lazia pay you for the Donnelly job? He's getting seventy-five thousand. How much is your cut? A lousy two-hundred?"

The air had been sucked out of the room. The prior conversations between the men in the shadows, ceased. They put out their cigarettes and listened intently. The man who sat, stood on his feet and made his way to the front of the room. He walked into the light. It was Paul. Sweat beaded from Sully's forehead as he struggled to remain cool. Harrison eyeballed Paul before continuing his interrogation.

"No need to sweat, Sully — we're all friends here."

"You ain't no friend of mine, flatfoot," Sully spouted under his breath.

Paul reached into his pocket and pulled out a pistol. He pointed it at Sully. Sully backed up, no longer in control of the interrogation.

"Is someone gonna do somethin'?" he screeched.

Paul shouted, "Is this the wet smack, Captain Harrison? That would be a yes or a no."

Harrison turned his attention to Paul. He calmly approached him.

"Paul, this is not the time. Against my better judgment, as a courtesy to Mr. Taylor, I allowed you to be here. And this is how you repay me?" Harrison inquired.

. . .

Paul ignored Harrison, raised his gun, and shot over the head of Sully. The room broke out in uncontrolled chaos. Bailey pulled out his revolver and trained it on Paul. The other suspects had moved away from Sully. Sully stood alone.

Harrison threw his hands up in order to regain control. "Everybody calm down. No one has been injured. Bailey, put that away."

Bailey reluctantly holstered his weapon. Several other policemen swung open the door and piled in with firearms in hand.

"Step back out," Harrison directed. "Step out." The officers did as they were told and backed out of the room, shutting the door.

Paul still pointed his weapon, "I'm waiting for an answer, Captain."

Harrison responded, "Paul, look at yourself. Who's going to watch over David with you locked up? You're all he has right now until we bring Nelly home."

Harrison took a few steps closer to Paul, "Believe me, if I thought it would help, I would shoot that guy myself, right above the sniffer, dead center. "

. . .

Sully did a double take.

"Hand me the gun so we can get back to finding Nelly. That's why we're here, right?"

Paul paused for a moment before handing the gun to Harrison. Harrison gave orders to Sanders and Bailey.

"Take him home."

Sully shouted, "Arrest that crumb."

Bailey and Sanders walked Paul out. Harrison handed off Paul's pistol to another police officer. He hopped back on stage and slapped a shaken Sully on the back.

"So we've established that you were in on the Donnelly napping, that you —"

"We ain't established nothin'," Sully corrected. "We had nothing to do with that."

"We. You said, 'We.' Do you mean, 'we' as in you and Lazia?"

.   .   .

Sully adjusted his tie and pulled it away from his throat, as he knew he had already said too much.

"Let's say I believe you, Sully. That your hands are clean. The fact still remains that we have one man dead on the street and a woman gone missing, along with a husband ready to tear you apart."

Sully looked around the darkened room. He could not make out the faces of the other men in the shadows, but knew there were some of Lazia's men lurking. He hadn't gotten this far in the organization without knowing when to throw a few crumbs and when to remain silent. A figure in the back of the room leaning against the wall, now stood erect and nodded once before placing his fedora back on his head and exiting the room. Sully took this as his cue. The entire exchange had not been lost on Harrison. "Alls I can say, copper, is that it ain't any of our boys." Sully wiped his brow with a worn handkerchief.

Harrison waved his hand, and all the suspects were taken off the stage. Once they exited, the room's lights were turned back on, and the floodlights shut off. The room emptied except for Harrison. Bailey re-emerged.

"Sanders is taking him home. So what about Sully? Keep him?"

"Let him go."

. . .

Bailey was confused.

"Lazia is not involved. They must be triggermen from out of town. They pulled off the Hart case, spent all their dough, and then got itchy for another payday. Donnelly will pay the check."

Bailey responded, "Think she's still alive?"

Harrison ignored the question and proceeded as planned. "Pull the Hart case. I want everything."

"Yes, Captain."

Harrison exited the room before coming back in. He held his hand out. Bailey handed over the half-empty bottle of whiskey in the palm of his hand. Harrison unscrewed the top and chugged the remainder of the booze before tossing the empty bottle back over to Bailey.

"You have a visitor," Bailey relayed.

SECOND CHANCE

*H*arrison opened the door to his office as Senator Reed stood, upright with an assertive and corrective posture, next to his desk.

"Senator Reed."

"Captain Harrison."

Harrison extended a hand to Reed, who acquiesced to the traditional exchange.

"I take it you're here for the Donnelly case? Please have a seat."

.   .   .

Reed ignored the pleasantries and got straight down to business. "Where exactly are you?" Reed requested in a rather stern manner.

Harrison sat on the corner of his desk. "Nowhere near where I want to be. We know they're not local and that they were behind the Hart case."

Just the sound of Hart's name stirred up strong emotions for Reed. "What else?" Reed asked.

Harrison took a sip of day-old coffee. "That's it ... except for the fact that we believe she's still alive."

Reed perked up, "What has given you that impression? The fact that a body hasn't been discovered?"

Harrison stood, "No, Senator. Just my gut."

"Well, excuse me, Harrison, but I require a great deal more than extrasensory perception, as does the Donnelly family. Have you exercised every avenue available, no matter how distasteful?"

Harrison shoved his empty paper cup into a nearby trashcan.

. . .

"May I be frank, Senator? There are only a handful of men in this department that I trust, and of those few in number, there's only one I can truly count on, and you're looking at him."

Reed reached for his overcoat and placed his hat on his head. "In a dire circumstance such as this, relying only on the trusted can be a hindrance and a crutch, held tightly by the powerless to justify their lack of headway."

Harrison was offended, yet held his tongue. "Good day, Senator."

Reed strode out of the office as Bailey entered with a box overflowing with evidence from the Hart case. He placed it on Harrison's desk.

~

At the farmhouse, Nelly was once again secured to the Larkin chair with her arms bound even tighter behind her. Nelly was blindfolded, although she had now memorized Jack's face.

"May I have some water?" Nelly requested.

Jack gestured for Thurmond to fetch her a glass of water, "Make tracks."

. . .

Thurmond headed outside to pump water from the well. He helped himself to a few glassfuls before returning. He pulled up a seat next to her and pressed the glass to Nelly's lips. She took a considerable gulp, which caused a coughing fit. Thurmond shrieked with enthusiasm as he pulled the glass away.

"Slow down, Dollface. Wanna drown?"

Nelly shook her head no, "More. Please."

Thurmond leaned in to whisper to Nelly, "If I give you another sip, will you tell me a story?"

Nelly was confused, "What kind of story?"

"Oh, the kinds you tell David. Just like you would for David."

Nelly hid her fear from Thurmond, as she didn't want them to know that the act of simply mentioning her son's name caused her great anguish and dread. Nelly wondered, *Will they harm David? How much more do they know about my family? What are their plans after they receive the ransom?* Nelly agreed to tell Thurmond a story. Thurmond rationed out a few more gulps.

. . .

Nelly's voice shook as she began with a story she had memorized for David; a story she sometimes whispered in his ear at bedtime.

"In the great forest, a little elephant was born. His name was Babar. His mother loved him dearly and used to rock him to sleep with her trunk and sing to him softly."

"I don't like elephants." Thurmond stated. "Tell me another one."

Nelly nervously cleared her throat.

"'Have you seen Tommy?' cried poor Mrs. Stout. 'I've searched from him everywhere, inside and out. I ran to the barn and opened the door, but found only chickens and nothing more.'"

Nelly paused and listened for signs of acceptance from Thurmond before she continued.

"I searched through the cupboards all over the house, and in the jam closet was a little gray mouse. I peeked under the table and threw the cloth over, and under the table was our faithful dog, Rover."

Thurmond lost patience, "Where the hell is Tommy? Tell me now."

. . .

Nelly's voice cracked.

"Poor Mrs. Spout was quite in despair, when she looked in the bed and Tommy was there."

"You mean to tell me Tommy was in the bed the whole time? Why didn't she look there first?" Thurmond asked, expecting a plausible answer.

Jack and Earl left the room to stand outside on the porch. Jack bit into an orchard apple.

"She saw my mug."

Earl listened intently.

Jack repeated himself, "She saw my mug and can identify me."

Earl chimed in, "Your face is a dime a dozen. She's too cloudy to point the finger at any of us."

Jack thought out loud, "We can't use the river. They'll be watching it. Guess we'll just leave her here, out back, under that pile of siding."

. . .

"Listen, Jack, we all agreed that as soon as we got the dough..."

Jack reached for his revolver, pulled it out, and held it at his side, with his finger on the trigger, "Agreements are for changin'. Unless you feel otherwise."

Jack glanced away for a split second and tossed the half-eaten apple. When he turned back to face off with Earl, he saw that Earl also had his pistol by his side with his finger on the trigger.

"I feel otherwise."

Jack paused for a moment before a smile suddenly lit up his face. "I knew there was a reason I brought you on this job," he said jovially.

Jack raised his pistol while removing his finger from the trigger. He holstered it before holding up his empty palms in a friendly gesture.

"If you have a better idea, Abercrombie ..."

Just then, Thurmond stepped outside.

. . .

"We're gonna be on the radio."

All three men rushed back inside as Earl put his pistol away. They gathered around the tabletop tube radio. Senator Reed was in the middle of a press conference.

∼

At the footsteps of the police precinct, Senator Reed lorded it over members of the press. Flash bulbs ignited and passersby gathered out of curiosity, while policemen stood in the entrance to the building. For an impromptu conference, well over twenty members of the press were there from newspapers and radio stations across the state, with even more concerned citizens, as they parked their cars and walked over. Nearby traffic was at a standstill, yet no car horns honked. Reed stood as a beacon in the center of the vortex, behind a podium with his papers spread out.

"Twenty-nine hours ago, Mrs. Nell Donnelly of the Donnelly Garment Company was abducted from our peaceful streets." There were murmurs from the swarm of people. "Nelly Don is not just another face in the crowd. Yes, she could easily be your sister, your wife, or your mother. In fact she is all of those things to her family, and one thousand employed workers as well. The Donnellys have single-handedly turned Kansas City into the thriving manufacturing center that our country has come to know. And how are they repaid?" Reed switched his approach to something a bit more personal. "David is her three-month old son. Her husband Paul is at home, taking care of David, awaiting precious word. We know these men are from outside the area and that they are linked to Brook Hart's kidnapping and murder." The crowd gasped. "All of America should insist, nay demand, in one collective voice, that the barbarous kidnappers be tracked down and brought to justice so they shall never again escape God's divine will."

A reporter shouted out, "Senator Reed, there have been many kidnappings of influential citizens. Why are you so involved in this case? Aren't the police doing their jobs to your satisfaction?"

Reed responded, "The Donnellys are very important to this community. They also happen to be acquaintances."

Another reporter jumped in, "Do you have any information on the abductors? Why did they target Nell Donnelly?"

Reed responded, "The truth about evil, son, is that it exists. Cruelty and envy are basic human traits stifled by most and replaced with compassion and empathy. These men know neither compassion nor empathy. The F.B.I. is offering a $75,000 reward for information that leads to the arrest and conviction of anyone involved in this heinous act against humanity. However, full immunity will be granted to the first person involved in the abduction who comes forward immediately and is instrumental in her safe return. That is all."

. . .

Harrison was in shock. He could not believe what he had just witnessed. This was, in fact, the first time he had heard of any such reward, yet alone one so sizable.

Another reporter demanded attention, "Excuse me. Excuse me, Senator Reed. How much are the kidnappers asking for?"

Reed turned to face the reporter, "$75,000."

Harrison pushed his way past the crowd towards his vehicle as Reed gathered his papers and left the podium. The reporters scattered, in search of the nearest horn to call in their story.

THE RANSOM

*J*ack cranked off the radio.

Thurmond looked confused. "They're offerin' our dough as a reward?"

Jack paced back and forth before he froze in his tracks.

"It don't make a bit of difference," Earl proclaimed. "As I see it, one has nothing to do with the other. It just proves what a valuable commodity she is alive."

"You're right. As long as we stick togetha, no one's takin' the rap," Jack spouted in a rare moment of agreement.

· · ·

"So when are we gonna get the dough?" Thurmond asked again.

Jack grabbed his coat and hat. "When I says so..." Jack left the farmhouse on a mission.

Thurmond returned to Nelly's side in anticipation of another story.

∽

Jack jumped into his vehicle and sped off. Several miles down the road, he decreased his speed to the legal limit as a parked police car came within view. He gradually passed them by. One policeman glanced up to see Jack. Jack tipped his hat as he drove past. The policemen had a quizzical expression on his face, before dismissing his instincts. Jack continued on without incident.

Jack arrived in town and found a parking spot. He climbed out of the car and wove in-between traffic to make it to the pharmacy across the street. He held the door open for a woman and her young son as they exited the pharmacy.

"Why, thank you. Thank the gentleman, Herman."

Herman eyeballed Jack up and down before exclaiming, "I don't like you."

. . .

Embarrassed, the woman pulled her son away and reprimanded him on the street. While the kid's gaze was still fixated on Jack, in defiance, Jack tilted his head back, raised his brows and flicked his fingers under his chin, giving him the old 'chin flick.' The kid stuck his tongue out as Jack walked inside.

The pharmacy, crowded and clamorous, seemed the perfect location to Jack. He could easily dissolve into the crowd. It also had two phone booths, both of which were occupied. Jack sat at the lunch counter adjacent to the booths. A well-worn waitress slapped a napkin down, then a coffee cup.

"Brew?"

Jack had his eyes on the phone booth.

"I said, coffee?" the perturbed waitress reiterated. Jack swung back around to face her.

"Nothin' for me."

The waitress turned to the cook, "This grifter is confusing us with a park bench."

The rather burly cook put down his spatula to address the issue.

. . .

"Listen, Mac, at least buy a cup of Joe or beat it."

Jack, eyes still on the booths, slammed a coin on the counter. The waitress selected a mug for Jack and poured a cup of coffee before putting the coin in the register. Jack took one sip before he spit it back out. The burly cook caught site of the spew. He slammed a towel down on the counter. The waitress calmed him down and told him the mug wasn't worth the trouble. The cook begrudgingly returned to flipping hash.

A booth opened up. Jack stepped inside and closed the accordion doors for privacy. The light inside the booth flickered on and illuminated him. He pulled out a handkerchief and used it to unscrew the light bulb until the light went out. Now in darkness, he reached into his trouser pocket for a coin and put it on the shelf. He went through his other pocket in search of an item. He couldn't find it. He got a bit agitated before locating a small piece of paper in his right front shirt pocket. He unfolded the paper. It was written in Nelly Don's handwriting. It read:

KansasCity
6-5122

He placed the coin in the slot and dialed.

~

At the Donnelly residence, police surrounded Paul. His son, David, had been taken to a friend's home for safety. The phone rang. Harrison placed headphones over his ears and signaled for the recordist to turn on the recording device. He also asked for the gaggle of officers to quiet down.

"Paul, are you ready?" Harrison questioned.

Paul nodded in the affirmative.

"Try to keep them talking as long as possible."

Paul picked up the phone's receiver.

"Hello?"

Jack salivated at the possibility of coming one step closer to the payoff.

"Paul, I want you to listen very carefully. I know the coppers have their glasses up to the door."

Paul responded, "No, I'm alone."

. . .

Jack shook his head in disgust, "This is not going to go very well for Nelly, Paul, with yous lying to me."

Paul quickly retracted, "Yes, I apologize."

"I would have expected more from a gentleman such as yourself. Listen, I heard about the reward offered. I want that too, see. It's now $150,000 for your precious dame. You heard me?"

"Yes, $150,000."

"Here are my instructions. In two days you're gonna go to Union Station, see, at twelve noon. Go to the North Waiting Room. You stand there in the middle of the crowd until someone slips somethin' in your pocket. You get on the train written on the note and walk to the third car from the front. Wait in the observation deck on the left side. Then yous are gonna look for two bonfires on the left side of the tracks. Once you sees the first fire, you toss the bacon from the window. Dollface will be at the second bonfire, waitin', once we get our dough."

Paul asked a question, "How will I know —"

Harrison grabbed the phone from Paul, "You'll get your money; just as soon as we have evidence that Mrs. Donnelly is alive and unharmed."

. . .

"Now who is this?" Jack asked.

"My name is Harrison. And whom am I speaking with?"

Jack cackled as he fancied himself too smart to fall for that old trick. "You can call me by my first name, IN, and second name, CHARGE."

"I've got a better name for you," Harrison replied. "We need that proof before the drop, or it's no deal."

"You'll drop the bacon out the window as I says, or I'll send Miss Nelly back in itty-bitty pieces. But not before we blind her."

Paul was beside himself. An officer had to remove him from the room.

"How dare you bargain with my wife's life," Paul shouted as he was being lead out.

Harrison was unwavering and had uncustomarily lost his patience. "I'll be damned if you're going to get a nickel before we know if any harm has come to her. That's it. That's the deal. Take it or leave it."

. . .

Jack slammed down the phone. The recordist shook his head no.

Harrison trembled with anger laced with trepidation. Did he just screw up the investigation and possibly cost Mrs. Donnelly her life? Was it all over? The phone rang a second time. Harrison picked up.

Jack relented before he again hung the receiver up. "All right. I'm a reasonable man. I'll get you your proof."

Harrison removed his headphones. Paul, visibly upset, grabbed his overcoat and headed for the nearest exit.

"Paul, where are you going?"

Paul flew through the front door without answering. Harrison pointed to Sanders, "Follow him."

"Yes, Captain."

Sanders rushed outside as Paul accelerated down the private driveway and onto the street. So many disjointed and ugly thoughts raced through Paul's mind. *The business will all be mine, but who would take over the creative aspects? Could I raise*

PATRICE WILLIAMS MARKS

David alone? Do I want to? Paul felt shame for these thoughts, but knew he has built his career and reputation on being a pragmatist.

He depressed the gas pedal and swung around a rattling delivery truck to pass it on the left. A farmer with a truck full of roving boys from the tracks, on their way to work the fields, approached from the opposite direction. Paul swung back into his lane to avoid a head-on collision and cut off the delivery truck. The truck driver lost control of his vehicle when his passenger-side wheels made contact with loose gravel. It veered off the road into a ditch.

Sanders pulled behind the delivery truck to check on the driver and boys. They were livid, but nonetheless okay. Paul continued down the road, undaunted. He had a plan to bring his Nelly home.

THE TRIO

*H*arrison, still at the Donnelly home, asked the recordist to rewind the taped conversation. The recordist hand rewound using a clockwork motor. He adjusted the phonograph cylinder and gramophone disc. The conversation was amplified through a cone.

"Paul, I want you to listen very carefully. I know the coppers have their glasses up to the door."

"No, I'm alone."

"This is not going to go very well for Nelly, Paul, with yous lying to me."

"Yes, I apologize."

· · ·

"I would have expected more from a gentleman such as yourself. Listen, I heard about the reward offered. I wants that too, see? It's now $150,000 for your precious dame. You heard me?"

Harrison asked the recordist to replay the exchange a second and a third time. Harrison asked, "Did you hear that?"

The recordist rewound the steel tape and cut his index finger. He quickly wrapped a handkerchief around the compromised digit and set the playback at the exact location Harrison referred to. Faint shouts could be heard in the background. He was able to make out the words, *"Hash over a barrel."* "That. That my friend is the sound of a lunch counter. Only one counter I know of that serves that 'slop over a barrel'." Harrison patted the recordist on the back in a 'well-done' gesture before he bolted out the door.

Paul pulled up to the front of the Donnelly Garment Factory. In haste, the front two wheels of his vehicle jumped the curb onto the sidewalk. He turned off the ignition and composed himself. He removed a handkerchief from his pocket and used it to wipe his brow. He took a comb from his pocket and tidied up before facing Nelly's flock.

News reporters honed in on Paul and surrounded the car. Flash bulbs popped and there were shouts which followed the mayhem. The reporters shouted such questions as, "Do you believe she's alive?" "Why are you coming to work?" "Do you feel guilt that George Blair was murdered for Nelly?"

. . .

Paul ignored all of their questions and strode inside the building. Paul had his secretary call for an emergency meeting. Every single employee gathered on the first floor. There were hushed tones, tears and hugs. Some were frantic, others solemn. Paul appeared at the top of the staircase. He descended halfway down before he halted, and then spoke.

"I am sure by now that you have heard that Nell Donnelly... my wife, your 'Nelly Don' as you so affectionately refer to her, was taken away by force. What you may not know is that George Blair, her driver, was slain during the abduction." Pockets of employees cried out while others were stunned and remained silent. "The police and FBI are waging a war against these miscreants. However, they are just part of the equation. I am shutting down this factory today until Nelly is found and the guilty brought to justice. Your pay will not be postponed, but will continue as if you had earned it. I only ask in return, that you, each one of you, search for Nelly. Search your neighborhoods, your churches, your abandoned properties. She is out there. Please, stay in groups and be careful. No heroics. Don't put yourself in danger. If you see something unusual, report it to the police right away." His voice trailed off... "She is still out there. We both thank you."

The employees dispersed. They grabbed their coats, hats, and handbags before they poured out of the factory.

～

At the Senator's estate, Reed was in his study with FBI Director J. Edgar Hoover. Hoover, known for his frequent outbursts, bellowed to Reed, "It is our duty to get the facts. The FBI does not establish policies– that is the responsibility of higher authority. We do not make decisions as to prosecutions– that is the responsibility of the Attorney General."

Reed stood toe-to-toe with the notorious director, yet maintained his composure, "Don't lecture me on the role of government, Edgar. When it suits your agenda, the FBI is both fact-gatherer and hangman. Many a citizen have found your noose around their so-called lawless necks for spurious activities."

Hoover replied, "My God, what more do you want? You have a substantial reward, as Mrs. Donnelly is significant to the prosperity of Kansas City and the country. But this is a war waged against the light. They have a specific agenda to weaken righteous organizations out of covetousness. If you get in bed with the wicked, you too will rise to new degradations. By doing so, you disgrace the profession of law enforcement by taking matters into your own hands."

Hoover paused while he unwrapped a piece of gum, folded it over twice, and popped it into his mouth. "If you go through with it, I will have the utmost scorn and contempt for you."

Barbara Ann eavesdropped from outside the door.

. . .

Reed replied, "That, of course, is your scripted public response. What is your private retort?"

Hoover rose, glass in hand as he was ready to leave, "Schemes of dishonest efforts by honest men belittle such men. Yet I understand your motivations. When all is said and done, I will give credit where it is due."

Hoover took a few steps toward the door before he hesitated, turned, and faced Reed, "… and hellfire where it is due."

Hoover passed Barbara Ann on the way out and handed her the empty glass before he retreated into the night. Barbara Ann shut the front door behind him and returned to the study. She placed Hoover's glass on a nearby table.

"Why in the Hell are you risking all that we've worked for?"

Reed, surprised by her tone, responded, "Excuse me?"

"I've smiled, opened up my wings, fluttering about to lecherous old men to fill your coffers. Now you're ready to throw that all away?" Barbara Ann stated in a raised voice.

Reed responded, "I have never directly, nor indirectly, requested you to compromise any part of your honor. In fact it is quite the opposite. Yet you repeatedly defy me for your own selfish gain. If you suddenly feel sullied, it is by your own hand."

Barbara Ann realized this heavy-handed approach was not working. She switched gears, "Listen, James. I know you are trying to right an imagined wrong with the loss of young Brook Hart. His death was a ghastly tragedy. But you did everything humanly possible to find that boy alive. It was just not meant to be."

Barbara Ann gestured for Reed to have a seat on the couch. He reluctantly obliged. She walked behind the couch, placed her hands on his shoulders, and tried to get him to relax with a neck massage. "Nell Donnelly is a lovely person. She is integral to this community. I understand all that. But even she would not want you to risk your political future for her. Perhaps, God I hate to say this, but perhaps, what happens is also meant to be."

Reed turned around, grabbed both of her hands at the wrists, and pushed them away. He rose from the couch and walked at a hurried pace towards the hall closet where his overcoat hung. He snatched it off a hanger, grabbed his hat, and departed.

NO HONOR

*J*ack arrived back at the farmhouse, full of energy from the day's activities. He was on fire, in the driver's seat, over the moon. Once inside, he confirmed the details with Earl and Thurmond. However, he mentioned only one bonfire, not the two he spoke of to Paul. He sent Thurmond out to gather wood for the bonfire, instructing him to load the back of the tin can's back seat to the ceiling, and not to forget tinder.

Thurmond asked Jack, "Should I include dead wood? Will it burn?"

Jack quipped, "Include it all. We want the fire to reach the heavens above and for the land to flow—"

"With milk and honey?" Thurmond added.

. . .

"No, wet smack, with money... money."

"Oh, oh, I done forgot."

Thurmond brought a glass of water to Nelly from the kitchen. He steadied the glass to her lips as she sipped.

"She can wait. Make tracks," Jack commanded.

Thurmond took the glass of water and placed it back in the kitchen before heading outside. Nelly sipped the water this time. She had decided that she was going to do whatever she could to help the authorities find her. She may not be alive when they do, but she sure as hell would leave breadcrumbs for them to follow.

Nelly thought; *The water has a distinctive taste. Growing up on a farm sharing multiple wells for drinking, bathing and cultivation, I know the more complex the terroir and the older the water, the greater the mineral content. These minerals are pronounced, telling me that the well has been sitting for over a decade. I'll remember this.*

Nelly also made it a point to place her fingerprints on every solid surface she could whenever she was moved. *Planes fly overhead. A fact that, at first, propelled me into a darker place. Hearing the sound of possible freedom, yet unable to signal for help. But I soon realized that there was a pattern to the flights; one in the morning and one at night. I would wait for the morning one to fly overhead, count down ten minutes in my head, then ask Earl what time it was. He found it an 'off' question, yet still obliged. I did this again after the evening plane; this time asking Thurmond.*

"It's 10:15 p.m., muffin," Thurmond responded. *He was more than happy to recite the time as he knew at eleven, I'll tell him another nighttime story. 8:20 a.m. and 10:05 p.m. These are the exact times both planes would fly overhead. This is good. I can use this to identify my location if I should escape — when I escape.*

It was like clockwork. Thurmond and Jack fell asleep around 11:20 p.m., while Earl stayed up on watch. Jack took the second shift with Thurmond relegated to the third.

At times Earl left Nelly alone to spend time outside on the porch. She knew it was more than just smoking. She felt this man may have been doubting his decision. *Perhaps I can use this to my advantage. But in the meantime, I'll take additional mental notes when the farmhouse is still. I know a mouse comes out the wall every night and makes its way back before 4 a.m. I can hear the rainfall on the roof, I calculated how many steps between the sitting room and the front door. I know that Jack sleeps very lightly and with his hand on his pistol. I know Thurmond often has nightmares and that Earl barely sleeps. I also know why Thurmond loves to be read to. He was never taught to read or write himself; he has others do it for him. Perhaps I can gain his confidence though the stories I tell him. What am I going to do with all of this information? Will I have the opportunity to use it against them?*

. . .

Tonight was especially difficult for Nelly. The physical trauma from sitting for eighteen hours tied to a chair was debilitating, yet it paled in comparison to the constant mental anguish.

Sometimes, Nelly tried to carry on a civil conversation with Earl, in hopes he would see her as a real person. During one evening shift, she engaged him.

"You are quite good at what you do," Nelly commented.

Earl studied her quizzically.

"You read about such things, never imagining you would be the headline yourself," Nelly superficially confided.

"It's just another job, sister," Earl stated.

"I'm curious. What do you think of Bonnie Parker and Clyde Barrow?" Nelly asked.

Earl put out a bud with his shoe toe and ground it into the wood floor, "They're a couple of discount, low-end, filling station car thieves who get off on killing."

Nelly was surprised. "Why do you say that?"

. . .

Earl explained, "They rob broken-down, rural, mom and pop outfits. Pathetic if you ask me. That's two crows I don't mind seeing 'em get what's coming to them."

"I don't understand. If you feel that way —"

Earl scooted closer to Nelly, "There is a hierarchy to this business of crime. There are those you look up to, try to emulate, and those that embarrass you, and bring shame to the profession."

Nelly sensed a connection forming, "How do you know so much about them?"

Earl continued, "Clyde wasn't always a two-bit'er. Our paths crossed at the Eastham Prison Farm. My father sent me there in-between school semesters when he saw a streak in me he wanted to squelch. Clyde was there after being caught stealing turkeys. The day before I was sprung, Clyde used a lead pipe to bash in the head of another man. That man deserved it. Been greasing his palms with Clyde's assets. That was Clyde's first killing. Now you can appreciate a man who kills for respect. But that Clyde Barker, the one I knew, is long since gone."

Nelly spoke as if in confidence. "You're a better man than Clyde... or Jack."

. . .

Earl leaned in even closer and uttered six words that left Nelly cold. "I am not on your side."

Though Earl was a step above the average hoodlum, he was still a hoodlum, only out for himself. Yet despite his words, Nelly sensed a break in his Gibraltar facade. It was just a hint of a crack, yet enough to give her hope, something to work with. Yes, although Thurmond was more attentive, he was also unpredictable and too eager to please Jack. Nelly decided that Earl was her best bet for survival.

THE DEAL

*R*eed arrived at the home of Thomas Pendergast, a sprawling estate which befit a man of power and influence. A houseman awaited his arrival. Reed greeted him as he was ushered inside the home. In the entryway, the houseman took Reed's coat and hat as he led him to the kitchen where Pendergast was making a sandwich.

Thomas Pendergast had absolute sovereignty over Kansas City, and he ran it like a well-oiled machine with his crooked ways and backroom deals. Pendergast, to outsiders, appeared to be a successful businessman. However, he controlled not only the political machine, but also the hiring of all city workers, all awarded contracts, politicians, alcohol, as well as gambling. In fact, it was said that if you wanted to get hired as a janitor, you still needed Pendergast's blessing. Although he lined his pockets from corrupt enterprises, he was also instrumental in keeping the city afloat during the depression. Pendergast, a rather stout man of sixty-three, greeted Reed with open arms. They embraced.

. . .

"My wife says I need to stop eating after 9 p.m. She says I could stand to lose a few. But I ask you, Reed, what is more enticing? A well-built woman or a well-built sandwich?"

Reed ignored the question, "I need your help."

Pendergast sliced the sandwich in half and offered the smaller half to Reed, who declined. Pendergast poured himself a glass of milk and took both over to the kitchen booth. Reed slid across from him as Pendergast devoured his meal. Pendergast spoke between chews. "I've heard you've put yourself in the middle again, making promises you can't possibly keep."

"What have you heard?" Reed retorted.

Pendergast spread a wide smile across his crumb-filled lips. "Everything, and more. Seventy-five K, not bad. Same gunmen from the Hart case. I hear Harrison is keeping details close to the vest."

"When has that ever stopped you from getting the information that you want?" Reed pronounced.

Pendergast howled with laughter and put down the sandwich.

.   .   .

"That ransom of yours has brought the whacks out of the woodwork. The station is inundated with calls, drop-bys, all promising to deliver Nelly Don... after they've gotten the dough of course."

"That's the price that must be paid, James."

Pendergast wiped his mouth, "Tell me Reed, why are you taking on yet another kidnapping? That's up Harrison's and Hoover's alley. You know it could be political suicide. And don't tell me that bit about wanting to make up for... blah blah blah."

"You have the entire picture," Reed offered.

Pendergast slammed his fist on the table, "It's just you and me. I want the truth. I won't lift a finger until I hear it. And I always know when I hear it."

Reed took a moment before responding. "You're right, James, to some extent. I do carry young Hart's tragic end with me." He grabs his gut, "... right here. It eats away at me like a parasite feeds on the flesh of a dead carcass. I looked Alex Hart square in the face and assured him his son would be brought home alive." Reed cleared his throat. "That was the second promise I've broken. I won't allow another."

.   .   .

Pendergast asked, "What was the first?"

"Listen James, I'm a proud man. I don't like to admit defeat. You know that. I've stuck my neck out for a family who has been instrumental in the success of this city. I personally have also made the acquaintance of Mrs. Donnelly."

"Is she worth sticking your neck out for?" Pendergast asked.

"What say you?" Reed responded.

Pendergast felt as though he still hadn't received the full story, yet was willing to aid Reed in his request out of respect, "What is it that you're asking for?"

Reed replied. "Her factory workers are out looking for her, so are the police and FBI with no results. It's time to liberate other 'resources.'"

Pendergast got up from the table and put his plate in the sink, "I'm surprised at you, Reed. I've always seen you as the cowboy with the white hat and shiny spurs. The kind of fella who faces off with all the evildoers in town; them with their six shooters and you with your wit and honor."

Though taken aback, Reed responded, "Honor is not so black and white, James. I think you of all people— Honor... it's still there, just under the surface, yet has the ability to take different shapes. If your honor is wrapped in goodness and decency, yet is *squeezed* in between the gray, it is still recognized as good and decent."

"That's what I love about you, Reed. Your fancy philosophies. But you're right, you know. I sleep like a baby every night, not because of my many good deeds benefiting my fellow man through job creations, soup kitchens, and the like. No, it's quite the opposite. Them out there, straddling the black and white. That's not me. I'm the gray. I control my *gray* world."

The houseman returned with Reed's coat and hat.

"What you need is right up Lazia's alley." Pendergast searched for something to write on. Reed pulled out a pen and a piece of paper. Pendergast scribbled a few lines down.

"Here's the code to get past the door. I'll give him a call and tell him to expect you."

Reed reached for the paper. Pendergast held on to it a moment longer and cautioned, "You realize that if it goes haywire, it's over for you. That's it. Your friends, colleagues, your backers that Barbara Ann so successfully brought into the fold, will vanish. And that will be where our association ends. You understand?"

· · ·

PATRICE WILLIAMS MARKS

Reed nodded in agreement. Pendergast surrendered the piece of paper to Reed who put it in his pocket.

"Some may say you've made a deal with Lucifer himself. And remember, I anticipate quid pro quo."

Reed understood, "Yes, I will be indebted. However, you should understand, that being pushed over the line once does not make a man a pushover."

Pendergast slapped Reed on the back as a sign of acceptance of his terms, "Don't think I've let it go."

Reed replied, "Let what go?"

"The first promise you broke. I have a pretty good idea. And you're going to tell me soon."

"Perhaps... when this is all over," Reed agreed.

Reed shook hands with Pendergast before the houseman led him out of the kitchen.

THE MUG

*H*arrison sat at the lunch counter of the pharmacy. The same waitress that served Jack put a coffee mug down in front of him.

"The usual, Captain?"

"Hi, Rose. You look stunning today. New hairstyle?"

The waitress poured Harrison a cup of coffee then leaned in with her elbows on the counter and hands under her chin.

"What do you need now?" she cooed.

Harrison pulled out a dollar bill. He gestured for her to lean in closer. He gently stuffed the bill into her cleavage. As his fingers lingered, he brushed both breasts before withdrawing his hand. Rose was turned on, but she'd be damned if she would let him know.

"Always going for the cheap thrills, hey, Captain?"

Harrison smiled. "Keep the change."

The waitress stood up straight, taking the dollar out of her cleavage. She rang up ten cents on the register and took the ninety cents and put it in the tip jar under the counter.

Harrison asked, "See anyone new today?"

The waitress responded, "We get town folk and strangers passing through on a regular basis."

Harrison explained further. "He used the phone earlier today. Didn't speak to anyone, didn't meet anyone, just in and out. A wanna-be tough guy."

The waitress thought for a moment. "Look around, Captain. This ain't the place for a Prince Charming type... present company included."

. . .

She continued, "But there was this real crumb who parked it, expecting not to pay the fare. But we set him straight. Only took a sip of the brew before he ran out of here after making his phone call."

"What did he look like?" Harrison asked.

"He was about your height, thin, thirty-ish, pomade hair parted on the side. Two-bit suit."

"Would you be willing to come down to the station and work with a sketch artists?"

The waitress smirked, "You gotta be kidding me. I can't afford to take time off."

Harrison offered another alternative. "I'll send one over to meet with you here. Okay?"

The waitress responded, "Just as long as he understands that I'll be working. I got three kids to feed, you know."

"You have a dog. No husband. No kids. Remember, I'm a cop. I can find out such things."

. . .

The waitress was a bit put off. "At least I got someone to come home to, Captain. And he is sure a hell of a lot better to come home to than a man working for peanuts, expecting you to be impressed with a ninety-cent tip when he's been gettin' free coffee for years."

Harrison realized he has offended her and backpedaled. He placed his hand over hers, "I apologize, Rose."

The waitress broke out in laughter. "I'm just foolin' with ya, Captain. Send the copper over."

Harrison guzzled down the last of his coffee. He stared at the coffee mug before he asked her one last question, "Do you still have the cup he drank out of? Has it been cleaned?"

The waitress searched through a tub of dirty coffee mugs under the counter before emerging with one, "This is it."

She placed it down on the counter in front of Harrison.

"Are you sure this is the exact one?"

"I'm sure."

"How do you know?"

. . .

Rose pointed out, "See that chip on the side? I gave it to him on purpose. He didn't deserve the fine china."

Harrison beamed, as if to say, 'That's my girl.' He removed a folded brown paper sack from his coat pocket. He unfolded it and marked it as evidence before carefully placing the cup inside. He sealed the bag.

"We'll need your fingerprints as well."

The waitress quipped, "That's what all the fellas say," before she tended to another customer.

Harrison exited the pharmacy and noticed that the sidewalks were awfully crowded for this time of day. They were women and children, mostly, with some men scattered about. And even more strange, they all seemed to have lost something. They looked into darkened windows and into shops that were closed or that had gone out of business. Harrison flagged down a group of women.

"Excuse me. I'm Captain Harrison." He extended his badge for inspection before he pocketed it. "What exactly are you looking for?"

One of the women spoke up, "Nell Donnelly."

. . .

Harrison was a bit confused. "You expect to find her here? Who are you?"

The woman explained, "We work for the Donnelly Garment Company. The factory has closed until Mrs. Donnelly is found. We've spread out across the city. We have to find her. She's been so good to us."

Harrison sympathized, "I understand how distressing all of this is, but you should all go home. We are doing everything in our power ... Your presence isn't needed and may hamper the investigation."

The woman spoke up, "Is that an order, Captain? Are we breaking some kind of law?"

"It's an advisory, ladies."

The women ignored the warning and continued down the street, searching with the rest of the crowd. Harrison, frustrated, hopped in his car and navigated to the police station.

Once he arrived, he noticed that Bailey spoke in hushed tones with an officer who may have been on the fence.

Harrison studied the situation before he called Bailey into his office.

Harrison served up a lesson, "Have you seen those people out there? Putting themselves in harm's way, possibly *tainting* the investigation?"

Bailey answered, "Paul Donnelly asked them to. But you can't blame him, Captain. He wants his wife back."

"Sit down, Bailey."

Bailey turned a chair around and took a seat.

"You'll never be an effective cop until you've learned to think, to react like a cop. Sympathizing with the victims instead of sizing up the situation and using an analytical process mixed with knowledge and experience, will lead you into a sort of judicious quagmire. Do you understand?"

Bailey nodded in the affirmative.

"Use your skills, Bailey, to form a viewpoint that ensures equitable decisions."

"Yes, Captain."

. . .

"So give me three reasons why it's not a good idea for civilians to get involved in a kidnapping case?"

Bailey thought for a moment before answering. "Safety, compromising of a crime scene, and endangering the victim."

Harrison was pleased with his response, "Send the sketch artist down to the pharmacy. Ask for Rose. She can identify one of them."

Excited, Bailey exited in search of the sketch artist. Harrison pulled out the brown paper bag from his overcoat pocket. He placed it on his desk, picked up the phone, and dialed.

"I got a set of prints. Yes, for the Donnelly case. Can you put a rush on it?"

LAZIA EFFECT

*R*eed entered an alley and approached a flickering light that illuminated a steel, unmarked door. Reed rapped his knuckles against the steel. A slot in the door slid open. The mug on the other side gave Reed the once-over.

"I'm here to see Lazia. He's expecting me."

The slot slid shut.

Reed rapped his knuckles once again. The slot slid open again.

"Marshmallow," Reed uttered.

. . .

The mug slid the slot shut again, but this time he unbolted the steel door. Reed pushed the door open and stepped inside. The door slammed behind him. He followed his host down a dank hallway, void of any sound. Once the door opened at the end of the hallway, life exploded in all its colorful glory. Liquor freely flowed, and a crowd of equal parts men and women carried on in conversation, eating to their heart's content and gambling, while a piano player accompanied a live stage performance with chorus girls on velvet swings.

Reed, of course, knew of these speakeasies, however, he had never stepped foot inside one before tonight. Not because prohibition made it illegal. In fact, Reed felt, this 'noble experiment' pushed through by the Drys and Anti-Saloon League, was not only a waste of time, but bred more crime, caused needless deaths, and increased the unemployment rate. The true reason he never partook? He was never a man to gamble in such obvious ways. His own cellar, filled with the finest spirits, was enough to keep him, Barbara Ann, and their guests satisfied for several more years. And since it was not illegal to drink alcohol, only to sell, they simply enjoyed it in a private setting. This was anything but private. Reed gazed upon the spectacle before him just as someone tapped him on the shoulder. He turned around.

A man, dressed in a black fitted jacket with long tails in the back, white vest, and white bow tie spoke, "Mr. Lazia will see you now."

. . .

THE ABDUCTION OF NELLY DON

The well-dressed man led Reed through the crushing, gay crowd towards a small booth in the back. There sat Lazia, as empty champagne and shot glasses surrounded him. A waiter refilled one glass. Lazia slapped the glass down and spilled its contents on the table. For if there was one thing Lazia would not stand for, it was spirits from a shop-soiled glass.

"Bring me clean glasses," Lazia pronounced.

"Yes, sir." The waiter quickly wiped up the spilled alcohol and gathered up the empty glasses.

A young woman of maybe nineteen, draped in a mink stole, leaned into Lazia. The kiss was not a fanciful one, but a rather sloppy, unromantic smooch. It turned Reed's stomach. Lazia spotted Reed. "Doll, scram."

The young woman scooted out of the booth. On her way up, she got a slap on the rump by Lazia. She blew him a kiss before she stumbled to the bar. Lazia popped a stick of gum in his mouth and chewed. From the looks of him, you might swear that Lazia was a simple accountant.

But Lazia, along with Reed and Pendergast, completed Kansas City's triumvirate of power. Though Pendergast and Lazia were corrupt, Reed balanced their control through justice. Lazia, also known as "Brother John," a legend in the criminal world, once received a twelve-year sentence for petty robbery when he was just eighteen. But he only served nine-months before his shocking release. At such a young age, he had already secured the right connections to manipulate the system.

Nowadays, he cloaked himself in a facade of credibility by giving away money he earned through gambling, bootlegging, and prostitution. Lazia was not above strong-arm techniques or the use of violence, many times using both at the voting booths to generate the outcome he desired.

"Have a seat, Senator Reed," Lazia said in-between chews.

Reed obliged.

The waiter returned with a tray full of sparkling champagne glasses. He placed them down in front of Lazia before he tended to another customer. Lazia slid a glass towards Reed. Reed picked up the glass and took a swig.

"What do you think? Class A stuff, right?" Lazia beamed.

Reed put down the glass, "I take it you've spoken to Pendergast."

Lazia responded, "A man who wants to get down to business, right away. I respect that."

. . .

"I need you to confirm that your men are not involved," Reed stated firmly.

Lazia smirked and leaned back in his seat. "Can I confirm, or deny? What is this?"

Reed slid the drink back over to Lazia, "This is strictly off the record."

Lazia confided, "I personally have nothing against the Donnellys."

"Then I can expect your cooperation?" Reed offered.

"Cooperation ... you want a hell of a lot more than that," Lazia chuckled.

Reed refused to have his demands open to interpretation or debate, "Send out your men by the car loads. Use whatever means you deem necessary to find her."

Lazia sat up in his chair, "Just four short months ago, you threatened to close my operations down and make them front page news. An example you said. Now you want me to use those said operations to help you?"

. . .

Reed replied to the accusation. "Four months ago we thought you were instrumental in putting one of your competitors in the ground and hospitalizing three others."

"And now?" Lazia questioned.

"Your hands may be clean of that matter…" Reed scooted closer to Lazia, "However, there are further enterprises of yours, less lethal, yes, but still explicit, that I can guarantee, upon further scrutiny, will not come out in the wash."

Lazia took the gum out of his mouth and stuck the wad under the table. The smirk on his face had evaporated, "Midnight tomorrow."

Reed corrected him, "Midnight *tonight*."

Lazia agreed, "Midnight, tonight. Mill Road at the fork."

At the police station, Harrison knocked on the laboratory door and let himself in. He carried a binder with him.

A lab technician gave an update, "We're almost done. We'll have something for you in a few minutes."

. . .

The technician used lycopodium, a very light powder. He covered the glass with it before he blew the excess away. What was left was an outline of several fingerprints. He carefully took a brush to further remove the powder from the part of the coffee mug without prints. He then applied some mercury and chalk to the prints to solidify them. What emerged were three solid prints, which stood out as strong as a redwood against a blue sky.

Harrison was satisfied, indeed.

The technician proudly announced, "I'll take the photos next. Hope you've narrowed down the list of suspects, or it could take weeks for a match."

Harrison opened up the binder where he had placed markers on seventy-three odd pages. Inside the book were profiles of criminals along with their fingerprints. Harrison explained, "None of these are home-grown hoodlums; all out of state." He pulled out a sketch from the front of the binder. It looked an awful lot like the man from the pharmacy. He pointed to the sketch, "I've marked the ones who closely match."

The technician knew the drill. He compared the fingerprints lifted from the coffee cup to the tagged mug shots in the binder.

Harrison placed a hand on the technician's shoulder, "It's up to you now. Find me my guy."

THE BLUFF

*P*aul and the family nanny, Margaret, drove through a deserted Kessler Park, a scenic byway that stretched from Paseo on the West to Chouteau to the East. They parked overlooking the limestone bluffs near a forested rocky face that descended toward the river below. Though it is too dark to witness the raging river, its vigorous activities can still be heard as it rushes past fallen boulders and brush. The winds bellowed and whipped the water as a ringmaster would a bullwhip. Yet surprisingly, the air was stagnant where the couple came to rest. This was the spot Paul and Nelly often enjoyed.

Paul switched the engine off. His intense stare at the bluffs was quite unnerving to Margaret. She didn't know quite how to comfort him. She knew she should either leave him alone with his thoughts, or distract him. This wasn't exactly what Margaret had planned for herself. Sure, it was a gas having someone as wealthy as Paul want to be with her, but she never fooled herself into thinking it would be anything more than an occasional romp. Yet, here she was, with him, while his wife was missing. She couldn't help but feel guilty. She actually liked Nelly and quite adored their baby, David. Paul placed his hand on Margaret's left knee. She moved in closer to him.

"Are you scared, Paul?" she asked.

Paul turned to face her. "You know what I love about Nelly?"

"Tell me," Margaret asked.

Paul confided in her, "She is the most brilliant business person I have ever come to know; man or woman. She's a better mother to David, than I am a father. She's hardheaded, a creative genius, and cares more about people than the bottom line. That is a trait, however, I take issue with. We would still be in that one-bedroom apartment making dresses in the spare room if it weren't for my investments. I supported her dream, I made it happen, I took our earnings and built an empire."

"No one underestimates your role in the success of the Donnelly Garment Company Paul, except you."

Paul retracted his hand from her knee and climbed out of the car. He walked around to the front of the car and sat on the hood. She joined him.

. . .

Paul convinced himself, "Tomorrow it is. Tomorrow, Nelly will be home... or..."

"Tell me, Paul. You obviously care a great deal for Nell. Why are you here with me? And don't fool yourself. Nelly knows there have been several before me."

Paul contemplated the question before responding, "Not enough respect, appreciation of how hard I've tried to make things right between us as a married man and a woman, and acknowledgement that this company was built by two Donnellys, not just one."

Margaret shook her head. "That's what you tell yourself. So easy to blame it all on the wife. I'll tell you the real reason why, Paul. You cheat because you're insecure. You may not feel as attractive as you once did, so you have to prove to yourself that women still find you charming and desirable. That's the real reason, none of that high and mighty hogwash."

Margaret hiked up her dress and straddled Paul by wrapping her legs behind him. She secured herself by interlocking her legs at the ankles. She clasped her hands behind his neck. He wrapped his arms around her waist.

. . .

154

"I find you extremely charming and extremely desirable, Paul."

With Margaret still wrapped around him, Paul swung around to face the hood of the car. He slammed her against the hood and landed on top of her. Paul reveled in the titillation of absolute power and control over Margaret. He dominated her by tightly holding both arms over her head with one hand as he used his free hand to pull her stockings down and remove her undergarment. Paul stood in-between her legs. Margaret allowed her thighs to be spread by Paul's lower limbs. With his tongue, he nibbled and sucked her earlobe before he plunged his tongue inside the eardrum. Margaret shook with anticipation. He ran his hands down her dress, ripping the buttons off the top and exposing her ripe, round breasts secured by a lacy brassiere. He shoved his hand down the inside of the bra, exposing a breast. Margaret moaned in pleasure as Paul consumed her breast while his free hand unzipped his trousers. Margaret, used to helping him with such matters, was unable to at the moment, as her hands were still held tight above her head. Paul reached inside his pants and released his manhood. He thrust himself into her with such impetus that Margaret shrieked in both pain and ecstasy. Paul forced himself deeper inside her; pounding over and over again, each time building in vigor and determination. Paul's brain shut off, yet he pushed past the sudden urge to let go. He held out for yet another moment before he lost all control. Paul then released Margaret's wrists and stood erect.

He adjusted himself as Margaret slid off the hood. She searched for the four popped buttons, yet only located one, near the passenger front tire.

"I'll replace the blouse." Paul reached inside his trouser pocket and pulled out his wallet.

"Are you serious? No thank you," Margaret said in raised tones.

Paul put his wallet back. Margaret picked up her undergarment and stockings from the frozen ground. He led Margaret to the passenger side of the car. He opened her door as she took a seat inside. He shut the door and walked to the driver's side of the vehicle where he let himself in.

While she applied lipstick, he started the engine. But before he put the car in reverse, he rested his head against the steering wheel, and sobbed; not full blown weeping, yet painful to witness just the same.

Margaret studied Paul. This was indeed the very first time she had seen him in such a state. It was quite unnerving, to say the least. She knew how to handle all sorts of men; shy men, unassuming men, educated men, prideful men, lustful men; but a broken man? This was her first. She did the only thing she could think of at the time. Margaret climbed out of the car and walked over to the driver's side. She opened the door and shoved Paul over to the passenger side. She climbed in, threw the car in reverse, and backed away from the bluffs.

THE FORK

*I*t was midnight, on Mill Road at the fork. There were no nearby homes or farms. Reed and Lazia met at the split in the road. Surrounding them were twenty-five motorcars, from Delanges to Bentleys, Cabriolets to jalopies. They formed a semi-circle in rows of five. The headlights were out. They were intimidating men that most would classify as hoods. All packed heat as they stepped outside their vehicles. Each motorcar carried four men each. They conversed amongst themselves in hushed tones. Reed studied the landscape, feeling a bit out of his element and wondering if he'd made the right decision. But he'd be damned if he would allow Lazia to read any hint of trepidation.

Lazia waved his hand once and immediately the men went silent. "We have four men for each set of wheels; that's one-hundred men. My best torpedoes."

. . .

"What exactly have you told them?" Reed asked.

"The first one to find her gets a bite of that fancy seventy-five thousand reward. I get the majority, naturally."

"Naturally. I don't want any unnecessary violence. We want these men to be brought in alive, still able to stand on their own two feet, to appear in court and be tried for their offenses," Reed commanded.

Lazia folded another piece of gum and pops it into his mouth. "I can't guarantee that, Senator. My boys work full tilt or nothing at all. This ain't no G-men convention. They get results by getting dirty. Yeah, some of them are real pond scum. But when you scoop up that scum, underneath, you see its caught a boat load of flies... simply by being scum."

"I'm not fostering any illusion of the type of men gathered here," Reed pronounced.

Lazia nodded, "Aces. We're on the same page then."

Reed took a step towards Lazia and invaded his personal space. Lazia spit out his gum. It landed near Reed's shoe. Both men stood toe-to-toe. The gathering of hoods moved in closer, in protective mode.

. . .

Lazia waved them off, saying, "I'm going to ask you politely to take a step back, my friend."

Reed responded with, "If Mrs. Donnelly is caught in the crossfire and is injured in any way by your men, accidentally, or intentionally... I will make it my singular mission to lay bare your vice operations; my reputation be damned. Do we understand each other?"

Lazia pushed the limits. "Wouldn't the citizens of Kansas City love to hear about how their hallowed Senator was willing to circumvent the law and negotiate with ruffians?"

Reed responded, "This negotiation may be in the dead of night, yet your actions and mine will see the light of day. I will see to it."

Lazia, a man who was not easily shaken, was taken aback by this bold statement. "You would be willing to risk your reputation, your Senatorial seat, ruined?"

Reed needed not verbally respond as the intensity in his eyes confirmed his unfettered determination. He removed the gum wad from his shoe and flicked it past Lazia. Reed turned and strode towards his car. "You have twenty-four hours."

Lazia waved the group of men in closer. Sully took his place alongside Lazia. The rest of the men surrounded him as Reed drove away. Lazia supplied more details before Sully and the men jumped inside their motorcars. The headlights flashed on. The motorcade pulled away, one row at a time until all five rows of vehicles were on the move. They spread out across the city in every direction. A gunman stood on the step outside each vehicle. He held onto the roof with one hand and carried a tommy gun strapped to the opposite shoulder.

Lazia headed towards his Buick Limited. His driver opened the back door for him. He climbed in. They pulled back onto the road and disappeared into the night.

Once the coast was clear, Benny the Boy emerged from a nearby field just a few feet from the fork, where he had been eavesdropping and biding his time. He staggered towards the road and contemplated just how this bit of information would serve him best.

At the farmhouse, Nelly's breaths were labored and shallow. Thurmond grabbed her by the shoulders and shook her. She was unconscious.

Thurmond called out, "Jack, she's actin' funny."

Jack, without much urgency, strolled into the room as if he did not expect an actual emergency. He too shook Nell. Nothing. Earl came into the room.

. . .

"What is it?" Earl asked.

"She's asleep. She's supposed to tell me another story. Wake her up," Thurmond demanded.

Earl put his head against her chest and listened for a heart beat. It was very weak and erratic. He worked feverishly to untie her from the chair.

"Keep those ropes on," Jack shouted.

Earl ignored the command and completely untied Nelly. He picked her up and laid her flat on the floor. "Get me a mirror."

Thurmond raced to the bathroom and elbowed a vanity mirror, causing it to shatter. He picked up a jagged piece and ran back to Earl's side. Earl snatched the mirror and placed it under Nelly's nostrils. For a few tense moments, the mirror remained clear, free of vapors.

"She's gone, but good," Thurmond declared.

"Shut up you dumb — " Earl shouted.

. . .

161

Volatile, Thurmond responded, "Don't you call me dumb."

Jack shoved Thurmond out of the room to cool off. Earl moved the mirror closer to Nelly's nostrils. Finally, a slightly clouded mirror. Earl again listened to Nelly's heart. What he heard was a beat that twitched and contracted rapidly. He knew this was not the normal heart rate. He placed the palm of his hand slightly left of her breastbone. He moved the palm in a circular motion, while he applied steady pressure.

"What the hell is that?" Jack demanded.

Earl explained, "I saw it done on the warden in the joint. I don't know if I'm doing it right."

Earl briefly stopped and held the mirror up to Nelly's nose once again.Vapors covered the mirror. Earl went back and forth between checking on her breathing pattern and massaging her heart.

Nelly eventually coughed up white foam. Earl sat her up and slapped her on the back vigorously. She opened her eyes. Earl wiped the foam from her mouth with his handkerchief. Thurmond leaned up against a doorframe and watched from a distance. Nelly tried to remove her blindfold, but Earl guided her hand away.

. . .

"We've come too far to have you leave us before the big payday," Earl said, as he helped Nelly stand.

Her knees buckled. He caught her. She steadied herself against a nearby wall.

"She can't be strapped back to that chair," Earl said to Jack.

"What do you suggest, Earl? We go out and get her a bed fittin' a queen?"

Earl thought for a moment before he said, "How about bringing some of that straw from the barn, inside?"

Jack gestured to Thurmond to go get it. He eagerly followed Jack's instructions.

"I hope you're not getting attached. She's gone tomorrow," Jack decreed.

Earl replied, "Just protecting our investment."

Moments later, Thurmond returned with a bale of hay. He cut off the baling wire with a switchblade and spread the hay out to make a mattress. Thurmond grabbed Nelly by the elbow and led her towards the hay. He shoved her down on top of it.

"I done good, right?"

THE FINGERPRINTS

*a*lone in his car, Paul tried to pull into his driveway, but was blocked by the Press. They pounded on his windshield, taking photos from every direction, and sticking their microphones up against the driver's side window.

Paul decided to take a few moments to speak to them; after all, he was not in a position to turn away exposure of the kidnapping. Paul cranked down the window.

The first reporter asked, "Have any of your employees come across any useful information?"

Paul replied, "Not as far as I know. But it's still early yet."

.   .   .

Another newspaperman, with pad and pencil in hand, raised his voice above the others, "Does it bother you that the police haven't turned up any suspects?"

Paul, frustrated, responded, "What do you think?"

"Excuse me, Sir. Keller with the Times. Have you thought of the possibility that Mrs. Donnelly may not return, and may in fact meet the same fate as Brook Hart, Abigail Redding, and the others? And if in fact, she is deceased, will you sell the Donnelly Garment Company?"

The mob of press grew silent as they awaited his response.

Paul cranked up his window, punched the gas, and muscled his way through the crowd. The sudden motion forward caused one photographer to lose his balance and he dropped his camera. Paul rolled right over it without hesitation. The photographer shouted profanities and shook his fist.

In front of the home, on the porch, several uniformed police officers were gathered in groups, conversing. They turned to glance at Paul as he drove to the back of the home. Paul stepped out of his car, leaving the car door ajar, as his thoughts were scrambled. Even the most rudimentary tasks were not connecting. He entered his home through the back door into the kitchen. Once inside, he tossed his overcoat and hat onto the kitchen table and strode in the direction of the bedroom.

. . .

At the foot of the steps, Harrison awaited his arrival. Harrison opened a folder and pulled out a mug shot, an 8x10 black and white headshot of Jack Oliver. He placed the photo on top of the folder and handed it to Paul.

"What's this?" Paul asked.

"Jack Oliver. The man you spoke with on the phone. The man behind Nelly's kidnapping."

Paul couldn't hide his excitement, "You found, her? You found Nelly?"

"No, Mr. Donnelly, get ahold of yourself. We haven't apprehended the gang yet. But this is very good news. It's progress indeed. We've got a name."

Paul slumped to the foot of the stairs. "What the hell good is a face if we have no idea where they're holding her?"

Harrison took a seat next to Paul on the steps. "This photo is now in the hands of every cop in the city, as well as the FBI. We know who they are. We'll still do the drop as planned. But we'll have agents trained on you at the station, as well on multiple trains. If he so much as shows his face..."

. . .

"What if he sends someone else?" Paul questioned.

"That is a strong possibility, Mr. Donnelly. But we're not releasing his mug shot to the press. He'll feel free to continue on as planned."

Harrison took the photo and placed it back into the folder.

"I'd like to go over the drop instructions with you again."

Paul used the stair rail to pull himself up. "I am tired. I have precious few hours left before Union Station and I have no idea whether my wife is still alive, or whether my son still has a mother. So until then, just get the hell out of my house. And take all of your men with you."

Paul turned his back on Harrison and took labored steps up to his and Nelly's bedroom. Harrison obliged and gestured for every officer to leave the home. They stepped outside onto the porch and joined the others. Harrison lagged behind.

At the farmhouse, Nell was wide-awake, while Jack and Thurmond had nodded off. Nell listened for Earl, yet heard no telltale signs that he was near. She also realized that the second plane had not yet flown overhead. So it had to be before 9 p.m.

. . .

Nell sat up on the bed of straw and felt the strength return to her limbs from the position change. She remembered Thurmond shoving her onto the bed of straw, but not much else before that. But she couldn't shake the feeling that, although her accommodations h improved, that her life was in even more danger. Though she had tried to make connections with all three men, her heart told her that neither Thurmond nor Earl would fight to keep her alive once Jack pronounced judgment.

A reoccurring nightmare turned on like clockwork the moment she shut her eyes. *I've escaped, I'm running, running, yet always end up at the same location; in front of a barn where Jack stands erect, feet together, arms at his side, like what you would expect from a soldier. The next moment his hands are wrapped around a shotgun. He doesn't say a word, just shoots... dead center. It is at this point where I force myself to wake up; at that exact moment every time.*

Nelly realized that this may be her last opportunity for survival. *These ropes binding my wrists are not as tight as the original knots while I sat in the chair. Perhaps the man who tied these knots wants me to escape?* She held her wrists slightly apart when Thurmond tied her up, but not too much so that he would notice. After twenty heart-pounding minutes, she wiggled and shifted her right hand out of the knotted rope, but not without a serious abrasion. This freed her left hand. Her ankles were left untied. Nelly removed her blindfold. Her vision was blurry and she battled the sensation of vertigo. She used the wall to steady herself as she stood on both feet. *I must fight every instinct to run like hell. Instead, I will close my eyes and listen; make sure it is the best possible moment to escape. After several moments that feel like an eternity, I open my eyes; take my first unsteady step towards the door. I try to avoid squeaky floorboards by pressing up against the wall and following it outside the room and towards the front door. One step at a time, steady; with each step I build mental, emotional, and physical strength. Once I reach the door, I stop in my tracks. Jack's revolver fell to the floor. Deathly frightened that the impact will awaken him; I squat down and wait it out. Though Jack stirs, he remains asleep. I rise once again, heart pounds, mind races. I reach for the front door knob.*

THE SWARM

*S*ully and his brethren, all men of the cloth, the Lazia cloth, covered the city the way the cops should have during their dragnet. Their flimsy attempt at a lineup to uncover the kidnappers had netted zero suspects.

If it had a back entrance, Lazia's men were there. Though Pendergast and Lazia had a finger on the pulse and bankroll of all things illicit, they left the operations to their subsequent owners. These owners, working in gray markets, could have additional illegal operations on the side that may have involved kidnapping.

Sully and his crew targeted every backwoods distillery within city limits. One, off of Peck Road, required a foot patrol most of the distance, as the nearest travelled road was two miles away. This was just one of over twelve they would visit tonight; and just another in a lengthy list of felonious operations sanctioned by Lazia.

. . .

These particular moonshiners, who concocted rum with unsavory production practices, sold barrels of rotgut to the thirsty masses. They made headlines a year previous when customers were blinded, had paralysis, and even died from their spurious liquors.

This was before Lazia took over the operations and distribution. Now this moonshiner followed protocols. He ground the corn into meal and soaked it in boiling water in the still. He added malt to transform the starch into sugar. After the appropriate time, he incorporated yeast, which kick-started the fermentation. The stone furnace beneath the still heated up the mixture to around one-hundred-and-seventy-two degrees.

When the pressure built, steam funneled through a pipe that stuck out of the top of the still. This moonshiner no longer used the "thump keg" method to create the alcohol, as those barrels were the reason for the rotgut. Instead, the steam simply made its way through the worm; a coiled pipe with circulating cold water from a nearby creek. It reached a final filter placed over a bucket before he was ready to ship.

The moonshiner replaced the filter on the bucket. He was so engrossed in his product that he didn't notice the men who approach from all sides.

. . .

Sully called out to the moonshiner, "Hey, come over here. We need to talk. And bring some of that bathwater with ya."

Sully questioned the moonshiner between swigs of rum. The other three men fanned out and checked every inch of the property.

≈

At the same exact moment, an armed second set of Lazia's men, rapped on a door to a house of ill-repute in a typical building on a typical street in the upscale Quality Hill neighborhood. The entrance was unassuming, though its architecture was that of the popular Renaissance Revival style. The inside had chartreuse-colored velvet wallpaper which draped the walls. On the ceilings hung chandeliers that rivaled a Royal's.

Awaiting the men was Madame Marquise de Pompadour; a refined, stunning redhead of thirty-seven. Though no one ever asked, she took her name and emulated the prowess of the mistress of Louis XV. She was both respected and revered for keeping the sordid secrets of lustful men.

"*Cette manière messieurs, messieurs* ... this way gentlemen," Madame Marquise de Pompadour purred.

She led the four men to the sitting room. With its Edwardian accents and a stained oak bar, it served as the perfect interrogation atmosphere.

. . .

"I ask that you be discreet; *respectueux*; respectful of our patrons," she requested.

Thomas, the one in charge strictly due to seniority, waved his men to gather the curb crawlers. The men raced up the winding staircase and kicked open the bedroom doors. One such room in use hosted a coat of arms above the bed. A Congressmen bathed two prostitutes in an oversized copper claw-footed tub filled with bubbly. Lazia's man grabbed the Congressman by the elbow and yanked him out of the tub.

"What is the meaning of this?" the Congressman shouted.

"Your wife's waitin' for you downstairs," Lazia's man pronounced.

"What?" the Congressman barked. "Here?" he asked in a panicked tone.

"Just foolin'. You should be ashamed of yourself. Now get downstairs," Lazia's man ordered.

The Congressman straddled the line between being incensed and outraged. As he stepped into his pants, "I'll have your head."

. . .

"Tell it to Lazia."

The Congressman froze for a moment, before he grabbed his shirt, shoes, and overcoat. The Congressmen, along with eight other clients of Marquise de Pompadour, were led into the downstairs sitting room where they were interrogated one by one by Thomas. The women gathered in one of the upstairs client rooms and were also questioned.

"We thank you for taking time out of your busy... schedules... to speak with us," Thomas announced.

The Congressman got up and bounded for the door. He was stopped abruptly by one of Thomas's men who stood in his way and cocked a shotgun. The Congressman sheepishly returned to a couch.

Thomas explained, "We're looking for some out-of-towners, men you may have come across, had dealings with, or even hired."

The men looked at each other in confusion. Thomas marched over to the men, unfolded a sketch of Jack and held it near each man's face. All of the men shook their head no except for the Congressman. Thomas excused all of the men, except him. They happily bolted from the room. Thomas stood in front of the Congressman, feet apart and hands in his coat pocket.

· · ·

"Who is he?" Thomas asked.

"What's in it for me?" the Congressmen boldly asked.

Thomas chuckled to himself. "What's in it for you?"

Thomas cupped both hands over the Congressman's ears. He slammed both hands sharply into the side of his head so that the compressed air in Thomas' hands created sharp pressure in the Congressman's ears. The Congressman fell, knees-first to the ground as his ears bled and rang.

Thomas bent down, face to face with the Congressman, "So what was your question again?"

The Congressman pulled himself back onto the couch. "His name is Jack."

"We know his name. Who is he?" Thomas responded.

"He's a lowlife that a few of my colleagues have used in the past for *'delicate'* situations. I've never used him, so help me God. I've never needed his services."

"Where can we find him?"

· · ·

The Congressman shook his head, "I don't know. But he's never far away from a simpleton named Thurmond. You find Thurmond, you'll find Jack."

～

Sully and his men left the moonshiner's domain and were on their way to the next one on the list, when Sully eyeballed a dilapidated billboard with a rather large shadowy object behind it.

"Pull over," he ordered.

Once the car had parked on the side of the road, Sully exited the vehicle. He studied the billboard with its advertisement for a shaving cream that had long since been discontinued.

"What is it?" the driver called out to Sully.

"Keep your blinkers on the road." Sully shouted.

The driver returned his gaze to the parkway as Sully walked behind the back of the billboard. He stalked the large object with caution. He saw movement from the tarp. He swung his tommy gun off his shoulder and, with a sweeping motion, riddled the car from hood to tail.

. . .

The other three men raced over, revolvers drawn, towards the commotion. They arrived in time for Sully to whip off the tarp to reveal Nelly's 1928 Lincoln Convertible. A possum, stiff from fright, or possibly dead, was rolled up in a ball on the floor of the vehicle.

"Call the G-men. Sully just bagged number one on the ten 'Most Wanted' list," the driver joked.

The men doubled over and howled with laughter. Sully opened the back door to the convertible, grabbed the possum, and rolled it into the nearby bushes like a bowler would a bowling ball. The possum, unharmed, scampered away.

Inside the vehicle, Sully discovered Nelly's purse and personal letter. He gave it the once-over before he shoved the letter inside the purse, as a lady's letter from her husband was all soggy in his opinion. The driver checked out the vehicle registration attached to the underside of the steering wheel. He confirmed that the car was registered to Nell Donnelly. The keys were discovered inside the glove box.

"Open the trunk," Sully demanded.

The driver exited the vehicle and walked to the back of the convertible. He tried several keys before the fourth one fit the lock. He popped the trunk open, then backed away. Not knowing the hierarchy in Lazia's organization could cost a man. He gestured for Sully to have the first inspection, and thus the praise or the wrath from Lazia.

"Who has the torch?" Sully asked. One of the men stepped forward, reached into his overcoat pocket, and pulled out a handheld portable electric light. He switched it on and illuminated the trunk. Sully leaned into the trunk and rummaged around before he pulled out a frayed rope tied in a hangman's knot, about six feet long, with thirteen coils. The noose was crimson in color, with what looks like dried blood.

NO GOD

*R*eed was neither a religious man nor an atheist. But given the opportunity to serve God or the people, Reed would always choose the latter. Yet there he stood, at the corner of Linwood and Broadway, at the Our Lady of Perpetual Help Church, a beacon to the community since 1912.

Reed was invited to the laying of the cornerstones of this church. They made it a grand occasion. Thousands lined Linwood and Broadway. With any parade and celebration, mounted policemen proudly followed a procession of Kansas City's Catholic elite. Bands roused the crowd into a crescendo before the official kickoff.

Reed attended the ceremony at the urging of Barbara Ann, who wore her favorite Coco Chanel suit; the one set in Chanel's favorite color palette; that of beige and white. Barbara Ann knew how decisive attending that event

THE ABDUCTION OF NELLY DON

would be to the both of them, and if a photo of her in her Parisian Chanel suit made the society pages, then all the better.

Reed shook hands, listened to obnoxiously extended speeches, and mingled with the masses, but he drew the line at actually stepping inside that day. For God, in his opinion, was void in such places. Their God was but a refined tool used exclusively for manipulation and greed.

Yet the name, *Our Lady of Perpetual Help, Redemptorist,* at this very moment, seemed quite apropos. Not quite ready to confess his sins, he studied the architecture, the blue-tinted Marian stain-glassed windows, the massive marble mosaic cross that sat atop the church, and the Indiana limestone. Reed grabbed hold of the door handle to the twelve-foot doors and pushed it open with ease. A gaggle of school children scurried past, freed from daily mass.

He took measured, hesitant steps through the lobby into the main auditorium. Not quite sure what to expect, Reed found himself impressed by the artwork and sheer number of pews set at an angle so not a one would block the view of the altar. Candles flickered in sync with the activity and energy of the room.

Unsure of what was expected or the protocols, Reed simply took a seat in one of the last rows. The seat was quite firm, and it would surely not sustain lengthy services. Was the church determined to make their parishioners' backends as uncomfortable as humanly possible to mirror Christ's suffering?

Reed shifted, in search of a more favorable position, when someone approached. It was Bishop O'Riley, last seen by Reed during the opening of the church. The Bishop, quite boisterous for a man of the cloth, greeted Reed with a slap on the back before he plopped down next to him.

"Do my eyes deceive me? Senator Reed. By the way, you won't find a more comfortable position, no matter how many times you 'turn the other cheek.'"

Bishop O'Riley glanced up towards the heavens, "I asked the powers that be for cushions and kneelers, even offered to spritz each one with Holy Water," he chuckled to himself, "but they deemed it wasteful spending of our parishioners tithing purse. But anyhow, so good to see you."

Reed spoke in hushed tones in the hopes Bishop O'Riley would follow suit. No such luck. "Bishop O'Riley, it is indeed a pleasure," Reed replied.

"Has the world fallen off its axis? What brings you here?" the Bishop asked in a non-rhetorical fashion.

"I can't answer that question," Reed responded.

· · ·

"Then you've come to the right place, Senator." Bishop O'Riley softened his tone and exuberant demeanor. "Listen, I haven't kept up with the papers, but I understand you're working with the authorities to bring Mrs. Donnelly home. Is that correct?"

"So far I've come up bare. And I have walked a shadowy line, Bishop, that will bring me either unparalleled satisfaction or ruinous destruction," Reed confided.

Bishop O'Riley took in the magnitude of the situation and how heavily it lay on Reed's shoulders. "I'm going to share with you a bit of Celtic mythology, with a story that was told to me when I was a boy. It's 'The Cattle Raid of Cúailnge.' Cuchulainn was the son of the God Lug. He was a fearsome combatant, though he just considered himself a warrior. Cuchulainn was part of an elite group of fighters from the ancient Irish civilization. He had the strength of the son of Zeus, yet, many times misused it. Some considered him a savior; others, a monster." The Bishop continued, "For Cuchulainn of Muirthemne fought many battles and defeated his enemies through cunning, strength, and determination. But that same determination would be the end of him as well. When his own mother came to him three times with a vessel of blood in lieu of wine, instead of heeding this foretelling warning of his impending death, Cuchulainn of Muirthemne declared, "My mother, why have you forsaken me?" She had in fact, not forsaken him, but had warned him, three times that death would come to him. Yet he stuck to the path he had chosen, until his enemies gathered around him and separated his head from his shoulders." Bishop O'Riley placed his hand on Reed's shoulder, "You have not been forsaken, and it is never too late to switch course, or ask the Almighty to lead the way."

Several pairs of footsteps echoed throughout the hall. Reed turned around in the pew to lay eyes on Sully and three of his men. The Bishop spotted them as well. However, his curiosity for their sudden appearance did not outweigh his concern for Reed.

Reed rose to thank and shake the hand of Bishop O'Riley. It was only then that he responded to the advice, "Cuchulainn of Muirthemne slayed many enemies before his prophetic demise, and not all with his mighty sword. He chose his final path, despite knowing the possible outcome. I've chosen mine as well. And though my outcome may be clouded, it has been laid before me. I need only follow its path."

Reed placed his hat upon his head and joined Sully and the others in the back of the church.

Bishop O'Riley had done all he could and left with the hope that Mrs. Donnelly would be found, but not at the expense of a man's soul. Reed approached the men. Sully turned his back to the Bishop in an attempt to block his view. He removed the hangman's noose from a paper bag and handed it over it to Reed for inspection.

"We found her jalopy; a real beaut. The noose was in the trunk."

. . .

Reed ran his fingers over the red-stained rope.

"It's paint. Fresh too," Sully offered. The driver tossed Nelly's purse with the letter inside to Reed. Reed went through the purse, taking note of the handwritten letter.

Sully added, "Keep it. Give it to the coppers. It's up to you."

Holding on to the note tightly, Reed asked a final question, "How many businesses have recently painted their buildings red?"

THE HUNT

*I*t was near 10:30 p.m. or so. Jack rolled off of the flea-bitten mattress onto the floor and stood up. He had to take a leak. He shoved the tail of his shirt into his pants and checked the chambers of his revolver before he shoved it into the back of his pants at the waist. He headed out of the room. Thurmond snored nearby, curled up in a ball in the corner. He used his jacket as a pillow.

Jack swung open the front door, fully expecting to see Earl on night watch. Instead, light from several lanterns glowed though the crack in the barn door. Inside the barn, Earl amped up the power of his punches to a fresh grain sack. He breathed out, which involuntarily flexed his abdominals to allow for greater rotation of his torso. With each exhalation, he grew more powerful. The sound of forced breaths during the punches reverberated outside the barn.

. . .

Jack was just about to step off the porch when a gut instinct told him to check on Nelly. He stepped back inside and headed straight for the sitting room. He studied what looked like her figure under an overcoat. Yet something didn't feel right. He walked over to the bed of straw and nudged it with his foot to awaken her. She didn't stir. Jack then went to the kitchen and grabbed a lantern. He lit it and carried it into the sitting room. He held the light over the straw bed to get a better view. Nelly was gone.

Jack angrily kicked the bed several times, which spread the straw around the room. He accidentally dropped the lantern near the straw. The straw ignited.

"Thurmond— Get out here." Jack bellowed excitedly. "Thurmond."

Thurmond stumbled into the room and used his coat to put out the flames.

"She's gone," Jack screamed, "She's gone. Finish putting this out. I'm going after her."

Jack loaded several more bullets into the empty chambers of his revolver, tearing out of the house straight for the barn. He slid open the door and fired two rounds into the grain sack. Earl swiveled around, more pissed than scared.

. . .

"She's gone. While you turned your back, she escaped. I don't know whether to shoot you now or —"

Earl grabbed his overcoat and rifle. "She couldn't have gotten far. I've been out here less than twenty minutes."

Both men flew out of the barn. Thurmond stepped off the porch and joined the two men. He handed them both portable electric lights. "Can I come? I'm better than a hound dog."

Jack decreed, "You stay here and make sure that fire is out good." Jack gave further instructions directed at Earl, "I'll take the path, you take the woods."

Thurmond turned back towards the house as Jack jogged down the dirt road. Earl, on the other hand, studied his surroundings before going off half-cocked like Jack. Earl bent down, searched for, and found a pair of bare foot-prints. He followed the prints into the brush surrounding the farmhouse. After making his way through thick under-brush, the footprints became more difficult to decipher. He came upon a downed tree. Nelly must have climbed over this obstruction as Earl spotted a thorn with a small splat-tering of blood protruding from it. Earl rubbed the blood between his thumb and index finger. There was still some moisture to it. He followed her same path and climbed over the log. Fifteen more feet and he noticed gravel with small broken twigs and crumbled leaves, as if someone had stepped on them recently. He sensed that he was close.

Nelly could not have travelled much further due to her condition.

Earl stuffed his rifle in a hollowed-out tree trunk and climbed up. He searched for a sturdy spot for footing and a secure spot for his hands. He avoided the dead or thin branches as he reached midway up the tree. He turned on the portable electric light and swept the vicinity. In the distance, Jack's light was on as well. Earl spotted movement near Jack, but he couldn't quite make out what was happening. For all he knew, it could be a skunk or raccoon. He shimmied down from the tree, retrieves his rifle, and silently trekked towards the movement. He turned off the light so as not to give himself away.

Earl paused at a patch of vegetation. No hint of it being disturbed. But how could that be when this was the exact location where he had spotted the movement last? He glanced around his perimeter in a three-hundred-and-sixty-degree fashion before his eyes focused on an immature hemlock tree. Its branches were bare, yet there was a hint of vibration reverberating through it. Earl circled the tree before he came to an opening. He turned on the light and discovered Nelly. She had crawled underneath. Nelly trembled from the cold.

"Come on out, Nell," Earl stated as he removed his overcoat. Nelly crawled out of the compact space, soiled, feet cut, and nearly frostbitten. Earl placed his coat over her shoulders. He then removed two handkerchiefs from his pants pockets. He gestured for Nelly to have a seat on a nearby stump. She

PATRICE WILLIAMS MARKS

followed his instructions. Earl wrapped one foot and then
the other with the handkerchiefs, securing them tightly.

"Thank you," Nelly confided. "You're not at all what I
envisioned."

Earl was perplexed by her comment until he realized that
this was the first time she had seen him. All of their interac-
tions before now had been with her blindfolded. Random
thoughts zoomed in and out of his head. He should have
been furious with her, yet he found himself strangely
relieved. Nelly could now identify him; yet that was not a
dominating concern. He had already set up intricate plans,
unknown to Jack and Thurmond, to leave the country with
his share. As an educated man, he had more options and
stood a better chance to come out the other side clean as a
whistle than the two louses he partnered with. Earl cupped
his hands together and amplified an owl call. Jack recognized
the call and sprinted through the brush until he came upon
the two. Out of breath and sick from an undiagnosed ulcer,
he doubled over and heaved. Earl marched Nelly out of the
woods and back towards the farmhouse.

The farmhouse was within sight. Out on the porch,
Thurmond sat as his legs swung back and forth over the side.
He devoured an apple. Once he caught sight of the two, he
jumped to his feet in a panic.

"Where's her blindfold? She's seen me, dang it, she sees my
face."

. . .

"Calm down, Thurmond," Earl commented, "your mug looks like a dozen others."

Thurmond scratched his head as Jack walked up the dirt road towards the farmhouse. Earl took Nelly back inside and tied her to the chair, but this time attached the chair to a wall heater. Jack scuffled in and wiped his mouth with the tail of his shirt. He outstretched his arm, pointing his finger towards Nelly. Nelly dropped her head down, avoiding his glare at all costs. She wept.

Earl moved to distract Jack, "We need to make like Weegee and take her picture. No drop without it."

Jack quickly shifted his focus and shouted to Thurmond, "Get the flash-head."

Thurmond left the room and reemerged with a second-hand Speed Graphic camera. Jack removed the dark slide from the film holder. He checked the bulb and focused the camera on Nelly.

"Look at me, dollface." Nelly kept her head down.

"Did you hear me?" Jack quipped. "Don't worry, I'm too tired to tan ya tonight. Tomorrow."

. . .

Nelly hesitantly raised her head.

Jack remembered, "Hey, where's the paper?"

Thurmond ran back out of the room and returned with today's rag.

"Prop it on her lap."

Thurmond unfolded the newspaper and stuck the top end under her chin as the fold of the paper rested on her lap.

Jack focused the camera on Nelly and the newspaper, cocked the shutter and then released it.

"That should do it."

THE IMAGE

"This must be it," the newspaper boy said as he found himself at the front door of a decaying tenement apartment. The door was cracked open, which he took as an engraved invitation. The newspaper boy strolled inside the dingy flat and searched room to room before he came upon a door with a sign that simply stated "keep out."

He pounded on the door with his closed fist, "Is it ready?" he asked.

A voice from the other side of the door shouted, "You're early."

The old man with debilitating arthritis worked inside a darkened room with one red light. His crippled hands, still able to work with film, removed a sheet. He used three trays of chemicals and water along with the seesaw method, something he perfected fifteen years ago, to develop the film.

He methodically immersed the sheet in a water bath. The film was now less stiff and easier to work with. Next, he submerged the image in the second tray of developer and again seesawed it to make sure every inch was covered in developer. He lifted the image for visual inspection with a magnifying glass, as his eyesight was poor. Once satisfied, he placed the paper in the third bath, that of acetic acid and a mild vinegar. Then came the final step, the fixer. He held the image under running water before hanging it up to dry with a clothespin. A weight was attached to the bottom to keep it from curling.

The newsboy banged on the door, "Have you got it?"

The old man watched as the image developed from faint, to robust, to a sharp work of art. He picked up a fan and held it a few feet away to speed up the drying process. The image was of Nelly Don with the newspaper under her chin. On the fence with the results, the old man opened the door, allowing light to fill the room. The newspaper boy stepped in. "It's a rush job. Not my best work." The old man turned the fan off, unclipped the photo, and handed it to the boy. "Careful, it's still a tad moist," he warned.

The newspaper kid flapped it in the wind before he rolled it up.

. . .

Angrily, "Is that what you call careful?" asked the old man.

~

At the police station, Harrison gathered a group of men into his office; a group that included Bailey and Sanders. "This is it, boys. Everyone has their assignments. Any questions before we head out?"

But prior to any responses, a front desk rookie interrupted, "Captain Harrison, this just arrived for you." The rookie handed over a rolled film sheet.

"Did you take a look?" Harrison asked.

"No, brought it over here, straight away," the rookie relayed.

Harrison removed the rubber band from the film sheet and carefully unrolled it on top of his desk. Though part of the sheet's image had transferred on top of itself; the photo was clear. The group of cops surrounded Harrison's desk in speculation. Harrison focused on the date of the newspaper. It was yesterday's paper. "And there it is," Harrison proclaimed.

~

Benny the Boy gingerly knocked on the farmhouse door. Inside were Nelly, Jack, Thurmond, and Earl. All three men jumped to their feet.

· · ·

"Shhhhhh." Jack demanded.

Benny the Boy walked over to the front stained-glass windows and tried to peer in. He couldn't make out the men inside, yet he heard activity.

Thurmond shoved a small rag in Nelly's mouth and pointed a revolver at her head. In hushed tones, "What are we gonna do, Jack?"

Jack loaded his revolver and tiptoed towards the door. He placed his ear up against the door in hopes of gathering as much information as possible. Benny the Boy's knocks became more aggressive. Jack silently exited the farmhouse from the back door. He made his way to the front, taking great care not to make a sound. He slowly poked his head around the corner of the farmhouse and saw a man he didn't know, but a man who was obviously drunk. Jack approached Benny the Boy from behind, cocked the trigger, and rested the barrel of the revolver at the back of Benny's head. Benny raised his hands and urinated on himself.

Jack was disgusted, "Turn around."

Benny the Boy obliged.

"Who are you? What do you want?" Jack demanded.

. . .

The front door swung open and Earl stepped out with a shotgun also trained on Benny.

"I'm ... I'm Benny, Benny the Boy's the name," he said as he lowered his hands down at his side.

"Keep them up," Jack barked.

Benny quickly raised his hands back over his head.

"I have some information for you... information you will find extremely useful."

Jack was skeptical, as was Earl. Jack demanded, "Spill it, crumb."

"May I?" Benny the Boy requested that his hands be allowed to be lowered.

Earl nodded in agreement. Benny lowered his hands and took a seat on the porch. He slowly reached in his pocket and pulled out a pack of coffin sticks. He showed the pack to Earl and Jack before he removed one. He lit it by striking the bottom of his shoe with a match, took two deep puffs, and exhaled. Benny came out with it, "You have Nell Donnelly in there, don't you?"

. . .

Jack and Earl neither confirmed nor denied his statement, though he stunned both men.

Benny the Boy made the zip motion with his fingers across his lips. "Don't worry, my smacker is sealed tighter than a nun's pucker."

"Give me one fine reason why I shouldn't fill you with daylight right now and wrap your pink neck with baling wire," Jack taunted.

"Cause I got simple needs. I'm no snitch," Benny the Boy tried to relay. In fact, that was exactly what he was, and Jack and Earl sized him up as one the moment he opened his trap.

Benny the Boy continued, "And I'm not much of a negotiator. How about I tell you what I know, and you decide what it's worth. Deal?"

"That depends on what you know," Earl piped in. Jack lowered his weapon.

"I know plenty. I know Nelly Don is in that house of yours. That all of her employees, about a thousand, are out looking for any trace of her. That there's a seventy-five thousand reward."

. . .

Jack raised his revolver once again, "If that's all you got —"

Benny the Boy grabbed hold of a pillar and used it to pull his drunken ass up to his feet. He flicked the cigarette.

"I got one more word for ya," Benny smugly relayed. "Lazia."

UNMARKED BILLS

*P*aul nervously walked into the bank branch that he and Nelly used for most of their accounts. He glanced around the lobby and looked for anyone or anything out of place. Moments later, Harrison strode into the lobby and took a seat. Harrison opened a newspaper and began to read.

Paul noticed a woman in the distance who resembled Nelly from behind. Was his mind playing tricks on him, or was that really Nelly? Before he had the opportunity to fantasize any further, the woman turned around to greet a gentleman. Of course it was not her.

Thurmond entered the bank after waiting outside for hours in anticipation of Paul's arrival. Thurmond feigned completing a deposit slip as he side-eyed Paul and Harrison.

. . .

A bank teller closed the shade on his window. He told his supervisor that he needed a bathroom break. He left teller row and found an empty office. He stepped inside and shut the door to make a phone call.

Mary Evans, the Bank Manager, was more of a librarian type than a bank officer. She greeted Paul with a firm handshake and a controlled smile.

"Hello Mr. Donnelly. We've been expecting you. Please follow me."

Ms. Evans led Paul to her executive office, the one up the stairs, at the end of the hall, with a view of the city. They passed by the bank teller, who exited a private office on his way back to teller row. Once inside the office, Ms. Evans closed the blinds for added privacy. Her secretary stepped in and took Paul's hat and coat.

"Can she bring you anything? Water? Coffee?" Ms. Evan asked.

"May we simply get down to it, Ms. Evans?" Paul asked.

Ms. Evans waved the secretary out. The secretary shut the door behind her. Ms. Evans gestured for Paul to take a seat across the desk from her. He obliged. She sank into her high-backed leather tufted chair before she realized that that action would not confer her intentions correctly; she intended to pay close attention. So Ms. Evans scooted to the edge of her chair and rested her elbows on the desk, with hands folded. "First of all, may I say how terribly tragic all of this must be for you. It has shocked all of us. We here at Interstate Trust want to do all that we can to make this transition for you —"

Paul perked up, "What do you mean, transition, Ms. Evans?"

Flustered, Ms. Evans explained, "What I meant to say, Interstate Trust is behind you... and Mrs. Donnelly, of course."

"I need one-hundred and fifty-thousand dollars in fifties only. No recording the dates and serial numbers."

Ms. Evans took a notepad and pencil to jot down instructions in shorthand. "Mr. Donnelly, that is highly unusual. It is standard bank procedure that we record such information to aid in the apprehension of such criminals," Ms. Evans explained.

"Unmarked, non-consecutive numbers," Paul reiterated.

Ms. Evans cleared her throat and poured a glass of water from a stainless steel pitcher into two glasses. She offered one to Paul, who refused. She took a sip before continuing. "Any other requirements?" she asked.

"A large satchel. I trust you have one?"

"Yes, of course," she responded, "we'll have this ready for you in a few hours."

"Now, Mrs. Evans. Now," Paul decreed.

Ms. Evans paused for a moment, as this was a highly unusual situation. But nonetheless, she wanted to be of assistance. She flipped a switch on her intercom system and called her secretary into the room. The secretary appeared.

In the bank lobby, Thurmond tore up the deposit receipt and walked out of the bank. Thurmond caught Harrison's eye as Thurmond forgot to remove his hat inside the bank, which made him stick out like a sore thumb.

Harrison moved away from the executive offices and followed Thurmond out the front doors. However, once Harrison stepped outside, Thurmond proved to be elusive. Harrison looked right, then left of the bank. Thurmond was out of sight.

Harrison retreated into the bank and found a spot to wait for Paul. Paul reemerged with a large leather satchel from the manager's office. He was rather controlled, considering the circumstances.

"Again, if there is anything else we can do for you..." Ms. Evans offered.

Patting the satchel, "For now, this is it," Paul responded.

"Good luck, and Godspeed."

Harrison joined Paul and escorted him out of the bank. Throngs of press greeted them with their microphones, flash bulbs, and questions. Harrison wondered how they could have been tipped off to their location. It must have been someone working inside the bank. Their presence only added fuel to the fire.

Harrison pulled Paul close as they made their way to the car. Harrison shoved a reporter out the way as he made room for Paul to get inside the vehicle. Harrison pushed his way through the mob to his side of the vehicle.

"That the ransom money for Nelly Don?" one asked, while another reporter shouted, "When is the drop?"

. . .

Harrison, tight-lipped, climbed into the vehicle and slammed the door shut. A reporter jumped on top of the hood, aiming his brownie camera directly at Paul with a bright flash.

Harrison punched the gas. The reporter tumbled off the hood and landed on top of other reporters. "One less vulture," Harrison uttered under his breath.

A partial smile spread on Paul's face.

FILL-UP STATION

*S*ully and his three accomplices arrived at Tiny's Fill-up Station. Tiny, usually a tongue-in-cheek nickname for a rotund man, was the given birth name for a wisp of a man, all of about five-foot three. Tiny rushed outside to greet the men.

"Fill 'er up gents?" Tiny offered.

"Check under the hood while you're at it," Sully added.

Tiny released the pump nozzle, removed the cap and plugged the gas tank. He immediately lifted up the hood and checked fluid levels.

Sully stepped out of the vehicle and joined Tiny. The other three men exited and cased the establishment. "Nice place you got here."

Tiny looked up, "Thank you."

"Fresh coat of paint too. What color do they call that?"

"Uh, red," Tiny offered.

Sully rattled on, "I thought it was a special color red, like the name for colors dames paint their pouts with. Crimson red. Brick red. Blush red. Well, actually, that's more of a pink. But there are many types of red."

Tiny sensed trouble. He closed the hood of the vehicle. He noticed the other men were no longer inside the vehicle. He pulled the gas nozzle from the tank, placed it back on the pump, and replaced the gas cap. "That'll be ninety-five cents."

"What about the fluids?" Sully asked.

Tiny responds aimlessly, "They're, good... great... no problem there, all full."

Sully reached into his coat pocket just as Tiny whipped out a small revolver from a pocket in his overalls. He pointed it at Sully. "I don't want any more trouble, Mister. Why don't you and your friends keep on moving," Tiny said while the hand holding the gun trembled from fear. He backed away from Sully and the other three men.

He turned and high-tailed it out of there towards the outside staircase that lead to his apartment, with rough footsteps approaching fast behind him. He took the stairs three at a time, with Sully's gang on his heels.

Tiny bolted the front door shut as the gang threw their bodies up against it to break it down.

"What have you done now?" his wife Gloria shouted.

"We gotta go," Tiny yelled to Gloria in a panic.

"Who are those men?" she shouted back.

The men almost had the front door knocked down. *Just need a few more heaves*, Tiny calculated, before they would be inside. Tiny rushed toward the bedroom and slammed the door shut while Gloria lunged behind their couch. The front door flew off its hinges and landed with a thud. The driver spotted Gloria, grabbed her by the hair, and pulled her away from the couch. She shrieked as some of her hairs were pulled from her scalp.

. . .

Sully exploded, "Where is he?"

"I, I don't know," Gloria answered before she fainted from the shock of it all.

"Let her be," Sully commanded. They searched the apartment and approached the only closed door. Sully leaned up against the doorframe, out of firing range. He knocked on the door. "We got your wife out here, Tiny. She ain't lookin' so good."

There was no response from inside the room. Sully knocked again, but this time, a blast by a pistol sent shards and splinters into the hallway, leaving a blast hole the size of a grapefruit in the bedroom door. The other three men leaned up against the opposite hallway wall with guns drawn. Sully gave the signal as the men faced the bedroom outside wall, took a few steps back and swept the room with tommy gun blasts. They shot blindly through the walls and door. When the dust settled, Sully kicked open the door and peeked around the corner before he stepped inside the room. Bullets had torn through the bed, windows, furniture and armoire, yet there was no Tiny. Sully and the men turned over the bed and knocked over the armoire. Still no Tiny.

"Bring her in here," Sully commanded.

The driver exited the room and returned shortly with Gloria, still a little light on her feet.

. . .

Sully planted himself right in front of Gloria, "Where is he?"

Gloria didn't say a word. Sully strolled through the room before he decided to rest on the windowsill. He spoke in a booming voice. "We know you're here, Tiny. Now come out or we'll have to burn this place to the ground; with both of yous in it."

No word from Tiny. "Burn it." Sully ordered. The driver struck a match and—

"Wait," a faint voice requested. Sully moved away from a floor rug that fell to the side when a trap door opened up. Tiny tossed his pistol out before he climbed out, "Please don't burn it down. This is all we've got," Tiny pleaded.

Sully gestured for the driver to blow out the match. Another man led Gloria out of the room. Sully picked up Tiny's pistol, aimed it, and shot Tiny in the leg. Tiny shrieked in agony as the bullet lodged in his kneecap.

Gloria shouted from the other room, "Tiny."

Sully instructed Tiny, "Say you're A-OK."

Tiny spoke up, while he applied pressure to his limb. "I'm okay, Gloria."

. . .

"That's fine," Sully added. "I couldn't let you get away with trying to kill Lazia's men, now could I?"

Tiny shook his head no.

"Now, we have an understanding, don't we, Tiny?"

Tiny nodded, "Yes, yes, we do."

"Fine. Now what did you mean when you said you didn't want any *more* trouble?"

"Just, just that I run a righteous business. I keep my nose clean; I stay downwind of trouble," Tiny lied.

Sully removed the lynching rope from his pocket and threw it at Tiny, who caught it. "What kind of red paint is that, Tiny? What would you call that? Looks an awful lot like the paint color on the side of your station; don't you think?" Sully whispered to one of the men present. He exited. Sully gazed out the window and enjoyed the gentle breeze. The man returned with a used paint can. Its dried drippings along the side matched the color of the paint on the rope. "Now I don't claim to have a professional eye, but it appears to me that we have a match. Ain't that right, Tiny?"

. . .

Tiny relinquished, "They paid me two dollars for some used rope. I said it had a bit of paint on it and it'd be better if they bought fresh rope from Anderson's hardware. But they said they wanted my rope. I saw no harm in selling it to them."

"You're right, no harm," Sully repeated. "Who were these men?" Sully continued.

"There were three of them. One was named Jack; he's the one pulling the strings. Another one named Thurmond. The third one, real quiet. Tall, top-hat type. Seemed out of place with the other two. They never mentioned his name," Tiny confessed.

"Where can we find this trio?" Sully demanded.

"Whatever they did, I had nothing to do with it, okay. I knew they were up to no good. But they paid for it, fair and square."

Sully repeated his question, "Again, where can we find these men? Don't make me have to ask you again."

Tiny thought for a moment. "I know they're staying at some old farmhouse. I heard them describe it with stained-glass windows they were figurin' on taking out and sellin'. Also said the outhouse was just a few steps from the porch, when usually they're planted out back. That's all."

. . .

"Would you know it if you saw it?" Sully asked.

Tiny shrugged his shoulders. Sully grabbed him by the collar and dragged him out of the bedroom. The other men led Gloria outside as well. Sully popped open the trunk and had the driver tie a gag over Gloria's mouth before he bound her hands and feet. They lifted her up and placed her in the trunk with care.

Sully spoke to Gloria, "Keep your mouth shut," as he slammed the trunk shut.

A makeshift tourniquet was wrapped around Tiny's wounded leg before Tiny opened up the passenger door to the back seat. Tiny was pushed inside. The men piled inside as well.

Sully took a seat next to Tiny. "Ain't nothing else gonna happen to you or sister in the trunk. We just need your assistance. There's a crisp Benjamin Franklin in it for you."

Tiny nodded again in agreement.

"We know every inch of this town. We're gonna drive you to each deserted farmhouse until you tell us we've hit the bulls-eye. Got it?"

A CONFLICT

*T*hey called it the Dust Bowl, and the devastating effects on Kansas' farmers had reached near-epidemic proportions. Although Senator Reed had put all other obligations, both professional and personal, on hold during this critical time of the abduction; this is one event that required his attention.

The community center was filled to capacity with multi-generational farm families who were pleading for support. They, as a rather powerful collective group, had implored Congress to pass relief legislation in order to save many from bankruptcy. Reed had gathered enough Senatorial support, yet Congress had refused to move forward without pork barrel politics.

Reed stood before the apprehensive crowd, with hopes that the words he was about to utter would assure them in some fashion. "I understand that most of you have suffered from short crops and even lower prices. Kansas has joined the rest of the Midwest in such difficulties. Gone are the days of wheat acreage increases by the thousands of bushels due to higher rainfall and mechanized farming. Just a few short years ago, you made a substantial living and were able to feed your families, your neighbors' families, educate your children, and set aside something for your golden years."

A farmer shouted, "We're down from one-hundred and twenty-seven bushels to sixty-two thousand and dropping. What are you gonna do about it?"

The audience applauded. Reed addressed the farmer. "What is your name, sir?"

He stood, "Sampson, Lloyd Sampson. Been tilling the land for thirty-five years and never have I been put in a position to beg. It's not our way. We make do. Only we can no longer make do." Farmer Sampson took a seat.

"Lloyd, I am here today because your livelihood and the livelihood of all the families providing for this nation is important to me and my colleagues. I hear you. I understand you."

Farmer Sampson nodded in appreciation.

. . .

"Dust storms on top of droughts are a mighty foe. You could say that Kansas received a double dose of misfortune and tribulation." The energy of the room shifted from apprehension to hope. "The Agricultural Adjustment Act will pay those farmers who have an abundance of crops, subsidies to not plant crops on their acreage. That simplistic notion will create more of a demand and will raise the value of your harvest. I'm not going to tell you this will happen overnight. But it will happen if I have anything to say about it."

The crowd applauded and stood on their feet. Reed moved through the throng, shaking hands and listening to individual stories. Barbara Ann also made her way around the room, speaking to those who were unable to break through the mass to catch Reed's attention.

After little more than an hour, Barbara Ann took Reed's hand and gently led him outside towards their car. Reed said his final goodbyes before he opened the passenger side door for Barbara Ann. Once she was in, Reed climbed into the driver's side and pulled away.

"The people expect a certain level of refinement, James. A driver is customary for a man of your stature."

"There is a certain level of primal control that comes from being behind the wheel, Barbara Ann."

. . .

Barbara Ann gazed outside, "I believe the timing is right to seek a higher office. Do you agree, James?"

Reed's mind was elsewhere.

"James?"

Eyes still on the road, Reed removed his reading spectacles and placed them in his coat pocket.

"What is the matter now, James?"

In a moment of weakness, he confided to Barbara Ann, "I can't help but think of the worst. What if everything we have set into motion is for naught? What if I've come up short once again?"

Barbara Ann slipped her shoes off during the drive home. "Must we revisit the kidnapping at every waking moment? The world does not revolve around the Harts, or Mrs. Donnelly. I'm sorry if that comes across as insensitive, but someone has to speak the no-nonsense truth. She may be gone for all we know. But the important thing is that you stood front and center, made pronouncements and came across as a man of action. Your poll numbers are up eleven percent. You held those farmers in the palm of your hand tonight." She paused for a moment before she revealed something Reed may not have been aware of. "There's even talk of you giving Hoover a run for his money when the time comes. You know what they say about every cloud having a silver lining."

Reed, disgusted with his wife, controlled what would surely be labeled as an outburst if seen by other drivers. "How dare you twist these two tragic events into a political opportunity? Who have you been conspiring with? With my sanity, my principles on the line, I come to you for a small piece of comfort. Instead, you book engagements, see opportunities where there should be none, and carouse with men of no honor. Don't fool yourself into thinking you're doing any of this for me. I have no such need for airs. You, on the other hand —"

Barbara Ann interrupted, "Don't you speak to me in such a fashion.You knew exactly who I was when this union was consummated. This marriage was not based on love, mutual admiration, not even convenience. You wanted the perfect wife to stand by your side, to look pretty, so that others would call you a family man; a man of the people. Comfort? You want comfort? I've told you to seek it elsewhere as that is not who I am."

The Reeds arrived at home. Reed parked the car. Barbara Ann immediately exited the vehicle, which was quite uncustomary for her. Their routine was for her to pretend to touch up her makeup while he walked to her side of the vehicle and opened her door.

~

But once inside the house, both reached the bedroom within moments of each other.

"Did you hear yourself, Barbara Ann? The woman standing before me is but a shadow of her former self. Yes, I know you were accustomed to finer things, and you are ambitious. Yet, do those traits alone absolve you of showing any empathy?" Reed asked.

Barbara Ann sat at her vanity and wiped away her makeup. "Empathy. That is what makes the world go round now, doesn't it? That and the manipulations of powerful men. I sit on the sidelines, relegated to following you two steps behind. But I have grown weary of that role. I want more. And you may be sacrificing my future, not just your own. You have attached yourself to yet another kidnapping, and if she's found dead, you will be seen as a failure. People don't re-elect failures. Pendergast doesn't get behind losers. It will be over for you... and for me."

Reed rose from the bed to stand right behind her as she removed her lipstick. "I started out as a man of ideals, strong opinions, and sometimes bullish behaviors. I have tried to remain so."

"And that may be the problem," Barbara Ann responded.

. . .

Reed placed his hands on her shoulders, "Is it too much to ask for us, on exceptional occasions, to step out of our set ways and give the other what they desire?"

Barbara put her makeup cloth down and turned around to face Reed, "What is it that you 'desire,' James?"

Reed walked back over to the bed and plopped himself down. With his head in his hands, he uttered, "An aspirin."

UNION STATION

*T*hurmond returned to the farmhouse and bounded up the front steps. Earl met him at the front door and let him in. All three men gathered in the kitchen, while Nelly remained tied up in the sitting room.

"He was there all right," Thurmond announced proudly. "Getting our dough right on schedule."

Earl asked Thurmond, "Did you speak to anyone?"

Thurmond hesitated for a moment. Jack jumped in, "Don't tell me—"

"No, ain't nobody talked to me. Just that copper staring straight through me."

· · ·

"You couldn't handle a simple job like scoping a joint?" Jack proclaimed.

"I handled it, I handled it. I left before he could get a good look at me. I swear, Jack,"

Jack paced the floor, "This ain't going exactly as I laid out. Just collect the bacon, dump the broad and easy street. That was the plan."

After a brief moment of thought, Jack announced, "We gotta change horses."

"What do you mean, change horses, Jack?" Thurmond asked.

Jack explained, "She's seen all our mugs, ain't I right?" Jack turns to Earl, "The copper got a good look at Pretty Boy Floyd over there, and Lazia is lookin' for us."

Earl surmised, "We have to look at all the angles. The drop is in an hour. We can do this. Just stick to the plan."

"Yea, right... we'll stick to the plan," Jack agreed.

. . .

However, Earl could read Jack like a book, and what came out of his mouth was exactly the opposite of his intentions. *This chiseler is about as honest as a three-dollar bill.*

Jack directed another question to Thurmond, "Have you finished building the bonfires?"

Thurmond avoided eye contact, "Yeah, it's done. Just needs a few more logs."

"Then you better take care of it, then get back here."

Thurmond grabbed a piece of fruit before he dashed out of the farmhouse and slammed the front door. That awakened Nelly from a groggy light slumber.

Jack turned to Earl, "Get her ready."

∾

Paul sat outside Union Station in the passenger side of Harrison's personal vehicle; a jalopy by Paul's standards, but a fine piece of mechanical craftsmanship to Harrison. Several plain-clothed officers in multiple unmarked vehicles were also present. They stepped outside their vehicles and entered Union Station.

. . .

"Let me go over once again how this is going to go down," Harrison explained. "We have you covered North, South, East, and West. I'm not going to tell you that we're batting a thousand; that things can't go wrong. It could. But you will only be a stone's throw away from one of our men." Harrison opened up a satchel to reveal stacks of fifty-dollar bills.

"This is what a life is worth these days," Paul stated.

"Some men value life in coins, not dollars. Keep your head on straight. Don't attach any emotions to the money or these men right now. I need you focused."

Paul closed the satchel.

Harrison handed Paul a newspaper. "Head to the North Waiting Room and stand dead center. Don't look around. Pull out this newspaper and keep your eyes on it at all times. You don't want to spook them. We'll have our eyes on you. Once they pass the instructions to you, read it quickly and proceed to the line. But before that, stand along a wall, ball up the instructions and let it fall to the ground. We'll find it and get on your train. Buy your ticket on the train. Head to the observation deck as directed; left side. Don't take a seat. Stay standing. Look for the first bonfire. Once you catch sight of it, toss the satchel. Then look for the second bonfire where Mrs. Donnelly should be waiting. One of our men will be riding with the Engineer and will instruct him to make an emergency stop at the second bonfire. Are we clear?"

. . .

"What if there isn't another bonfire?" Paul questioned.

"Then we continue with our investigation. We'll trace the notes and go from there."

"Wait, I asked for clean bills," Paul exclaimed.

Harrison let him in, "We couldn't take that chance."

Paul climbed out of the car and slammed the door shut. "If marked bills get Nelly killed, I'm coming after you."

With that, Paul marched into Union Station. Harrison allowed Paul to get twenty feet away before he tailed him inside.

Paul gazed upon many of the thousands of travelers sprawled across the station's eight hundred and fifty-thousand square feet, nine hundred rooms, and ten stories. He passed through her arched entrance, which led to the large matching arched windows, marble floors, and thirty-five hundred pound chandeliers.

But Paul was only interested in one marvel: that of the clock which hung above, in the center of the station and stretched six feet in diameter. It read 11:32 a.m. As instructed, Paul walked the quarter mile stretch towards North Station. He passed Harvey House Restaurant, cigar shops, pharmacies, buy bond booths, barbershops, and the railroad office.

Once he reached the North Station, which could easily hold ten thousand people, Paul pushed his way through the crowd to the dead center of the space. Above him were ninety-five foot high ceilings. The crowds, the ceilings, and the satchel overwhelmed Paul. He lost his balance and could easily have fallen and been trampled on if it weren't for a stranger who caught him.

Paul panicked, 'Is this him?' he thought to himself. The man quickly disappeared into the crowd. Paul checked his pockets — no notes. It was not him. Though instructed not to, Paul searched the vast room for a sign that he was being watched. *There, by the bonds shop... that must be one of Harrison's. He is getting his shoes shined... he hasn't taken his eyes off of me.* Feeling a bit more at ease, Paul pulled out his newspaper and read it folded, as there was no room to open the paper within the crushing crowds. He planted his feet and began the torturous waiting game.

Paul pulled out his pocket watch. It's 11:58 a.m. No sign of them. 11:59, 12:01. *Where the hell are they? Did they make Harrison's men? Is it too hot and they skipped town?* All these thoughts and more raced through Paul's mind.

Paul caught a glimpse of Harrison from the corner of his eye, in a phone booth. Paul dropped his newspaper while he re-checked his pocket watch. The newspaper landed on the tile floor and flopped open. Inside was a note. Paul quickly picked up the newspaper and note and moved away from the crowds. He was right. The man who kept him from falling was his contact. He struggled to remember his features. *Was he 5'7 or 5'11? Brown or black hair? Round or square jawed?* His mind was a blank.

He opened the note and it simply stated:

Rail 64 Car 3

Paul scanned the station signs and honed in on Rail 64. He had no idea where it was going, and didn't care. He balled up the note and let it fall to the ground. He weaved through the crowd as quickly as possible to catch the train at Rail 64 before it departed at 12:10 p.m. exactly.

RAIL 64

*D*espite having over fifteen agents with eyes on Paul Donnelly, Harrison failed at identifying the contact. Nonetheless, Harrison knew that there wasn't time to dwell on mistakes. He picked up the crumpled piece of paper Paul left behind and quickly followed him.

The crowd of travelers seemed to part miraculously as Harrison and his team darted towards Rail 64. They had but moments as the train was already pulling away from the station. Harrison ran alongside the locomotive, grabbed hold of a rail, and hoisted himself on board. But not before he slammed into the side. His revolver dislodged and dropped between the tracks. Three of his men made it on board as well at different locations. Harrison landed in the tenth car. Battered and bruised, he passed through one car after another until he settled on the third. He ignored his cracked ribs and wrist sprain as what was most important at this moment was protecting Paul.

. . .

Once the tracks were clear and the train out of sight, Earl jumped down between the rails and retrieved Harrison's revolver.

Harrison spotted Paul in the third car, the observation deck. Paul clutched his satchel and leaned next to a partially opened window. Harrison grabbed a cloth napkin from a tray carried by a server. He used it to wipe his brows. He took an open seat on the same side of the train where Paul planted himself, just a few rows behind. Although the instructions led Harrison to believe the contact would not be on the train, he wasn't taking any chances. He treated everyone in Car Three as a suspect. Harrison pulled down his window to allow a cool breeze in. The train Conductor came through and collected tickets. Harrison paid for his in cash. He received a punched card. A few rows up, Paul reached into his pocket and paid for his ticket as well.

A young man of about seventeen sat next to Harrison and tried to make conversation. "You know if you pay for your ticket at the counter, they give senior rates. You can only get it there," the teen shared.

Harrison removed his hat, "Thanks for the tip. Now take a powder."

Miffed, the teen got up and located another seat. Harrison couldn't afford any distractions. He placed his hat and jacket on the seat next to him to signify that the seat was taken.

Two of Harrison's men arrived and positioned themselves in front of and behind Paul.

Harrison stuck his head out the window and sniffed the air. He believed he could smell smoke, possibly from a bonfire. But he couldn't be sure until they got closer.

Harrison had always had a keen sense of smell, which proved to be an annoyance to his siblings when growing up. Rations were tight during his childhood. His parents always made sure things were divided up equally between the three of them. However, when one child snuck an extra helping, or brought a piece of candy home, they could never hide it from Harrison. He could tell you in which pocket the gum drop was located, along with what flavor it was, and even if it had been licked or not. His family even joked that he could identify what a person ate a week ago for breakfast.

Now he called on his penetrating scent detection to identify a bonfire. He inhaled once again and calculated that it was just under two miles away. He flicked a finger past his nose. One of his men got up and walked up to Paul. He gently tapped him on the arm as he passed. Paul inched closer to the window in anticipation.

Another mile had come and gone. Just one more. Harrison rose to his feet to get a better look as they approached puffs of smoke ascending towards the heavens. *This is it*, he thought.

. . .

The bonfire burned bright and strong. It was set around fifty feet away from the railroad tracks. Other passengers noticed it upon their approach, but it didn't command their attention. They simply went back to whatever it was they were doing.

The train was less than two hundred feet away from the bonfire. Paul shoved the window down as far as it could go. One hundred feet away. Paul checked the lock on the satchel. Fifty feet away. Paul bowed his head, as if in prayer. Twenty feet away... Paul heaved the satchel out the window. The satchel flipped several times before it landed in a thistle bush.

The teen rushed to Paul's side, "What did you do that for?"

Paul stuck his head out the window and looked forward in anticipation of the second bonfire where Nelly should be. Harrison locked his eyes on the satchel as a man stepped out of the nearby forest and retrieved the satchel. Once the satchel and man were out of view, Harrison watched for the second bonfire as well.

Although they had complied with the kidnappers' instructions, Harrison had a gut feeling that it was not quite over.

Harrison estimated that they had covered another eight miles. They should be approaching the second bonfire shortly. All the hours spent on this case could culminate in a successful conclusion in just a few minutes. That was his hope, but his sense of smell did not detect a second bonfire. He kept his concerns to himself until it became evident to Paul as well.

The train flew past an unlit pile of logs and twigs. It had been made in the same fashion as the first. However, Nelly was nowhere to be found.

Harrison's gut proved true-to-form once again, although he wished he were wrong in this case.

Paul screamed out in anguish as he held onto the open window in a death grip. Other passengers, caught off guard, froze in their seats. The teen inched away from Paul and retreated to the back of the train car in fear. Harrison came behind Paul and pried his hands away from the window. Paul flopped into a seat. Harrison took the seat next to him without any words exchanged.

OSTRICH FARM

*E*arl held the satchel close to his body the way a football player carried a ball towards the end zone. Thurmond trailed behind him, just a few short feet away. They trekked through the dense brush. Earl used his free hand to snap low branches and swipe away at other foliage obstacles.

"Let's check," Thurmond requested.

Earl turned around to face Thurmond. He unlatched the satchel and opened it up. Inside, Nirvana.

"How much you suppose?"

"One-hundred and fifty-thousand," Earl replied.

. . .

"Can I hold it?"

Earl closed the satchel and continued through the brush until they reached their car. Thurmond climbed into the driver's side.

Once on the road, "What 'cha gonna do with yours?" Thurmond asked Earl.

Earl fantasized for a moment. "Go somewhere warm. What about you?"

Thurmond blurted out his intentions right away, "I'm gonna start my own business. An ostrich farm."

Earl looked at him to see if he was serious.

"I heard about one in Lincoln Park, California. They got ostrich's for eatin', for a petting zoo, for pulling carts. They call them birds; they are birds, you know, even though they can't fly. They call them the most innocently powerful and most powerful innocents. I kinda feel a kinship toward them; though I never seen one in person. So I figured I'd get two of them; a male and a female. They cost around eight G's each, you know. I'd carry their eggs around in a wheel barrel. Ain't that funny, eggs in a wheel barrel on a cause of them being humongous. And I'd figure on trainin' em so ladies could ride them side saddle with a harness, then pick their feathers for a hat. Maybe I'll even find a jockey to ride it and beat the world record for fastest ostrich."

Earl listened intently but didn't fully believe what was coming out of Thurmond's mouth.

"But you know the best thing about ostriches?" Thurmond asked, fully expecting an "I don't know" from Earl.

"That they have a mean streak?" Earl offered.

Thurmond, a bit upset, "Yeah, that, but the best part... they have a kick that can kill. Imagine that, being able to kill a man with a kick. And it don't have to be in the head neither."

"Sounds like you have it all figured out, Thurmond."

Thurmond pulled out a piece of paper from his pocket and handed it to Earl. Earl unfolded the tattered paper and read it. It read:

Cost Breakdown
    Two African ostriches: sixteen thousand
    One acre of farmland in California:
    three hundred and twenty-six
    Coops and fences: one hundred and ninety-nine
    Tent and outhouse: seventy-five dollars

Charge admission, ten cents each

Earl could not help but be impressed with Thurmond's thought-out plan. "How long does it take for an egg to hatch?" Earl asked.

Thurmond scratched his head, grabbed the paper, and stuffed it back inside his coat pocket. They pulled up outside the farmhouse where Jack, with a wide stance, awaited their arrival.

Thurmond turned off the ignition, "Don't tell Jack."

Earl grabbed the keys from the ignition and climbed out of the car.

"Promise?" Thurmond asked.

Earl nodded his head before he met Jack on the porch. They headed inside. Thurmond followed.

In the kitchen, Earl removed the money from the satchel and stacked the fifty-dollar bills in neat rows on the kitchen table. Jack counted out loud each bundle and recorded each with a simple pencil mark.

. . .

"One-hundred and forty-seven thousand, one-hundred and forty-eight thousand, one-hundred and forty-nine thousand... one-hundred and fifty G's."

"I've never seen so much money in my whole life," Thurmond exclaimed. "Can I have my cut now?"

Jack divvied up the cash and gave himself ninety-five thousand, and Thurmond and Earl were to split the rest.

"I thought I was to get twenty percent," Thurmond complained.

"Do you even know what twenty percent is?" Jack sarcastically asked.

"I do," commented Earl, as he took five-thousand from Jack's pile. He gave Thurmond thirty-thousand. He kept thirty-thousand for himself.

Jack snatched the leather satchel and stuffed his money inside.

"So what we gonna do with Mrs. Nelly now that we couldn't leave her at the second bonfire?" Thurmond wanted to know.

· · ·

Earl jumped in, "We have our money. Let's leave her be. Once we're out of the county, call the coppers and tell them where she is."

"Dollface can draw a road map of our mugs. I ain't gonna let that happen. I plan on spending this bacon... every last dollar," Jack pronounced.

"Yeah, she could squeal," Thurmond chimed in.

Earl stuffed his dough into his jacket and pants pockets before he headed to the sitting room where Nelly was tied up and loosened her bindings.

Nelly raised her head; a difficult task as she had not eaten or had anything to drink for over twelve hours. Her mind could not remember the last time a plane had flown overhead. What she could see, however, was stacks of money in Thurmond's hands as he entered the room behind Jack.

Nelly's mind focused. *I guess this is it. I have to fight, I have to. If I could just reach one of their guns, I would empty it into Jack. Oh, God, I can't feel my legs... my arms are numb. Am I even alive?*

"What do you think you're doing?" Jack demanded.

"I can't let you do it, Jack."

.   .   .

Jack dropped his satchel full of cash and hovered his hand near his revolver, "Can't let me do what, Earl?"

Earl untied Nelly.

Jack raised his voice, "You shouldn't have done that."

Earl lifted Nelly to her feet and leaned her up against him. Her legs were like jelly.

"Don't mess things up for me, Earl," Thurmond shouted.

Earl pulled out his revolver from his back holster and cocked the trigger. With the other hand, he steadied Nelly as they took a few short steps.

Earl tried to reason with Jack. "Have some honor. We have what we want. So what if she saw our faces? By the time we're identified, we'll be six states over. I'm gonna drop her off at the doctor's doorstep. That's it." Earl and Nelly took several more tiny steps towards the front door.

"I can't let you two leave. I'm not going back inside," Jack shouted.

.   .   .

Earl and Nelly were at the front door. Jack raised his weapon. Thurmond had come from around the corner hell-bent on dragging Nelly back, even if that meant givin' it to Earl. He lunged towards Earl and Nelly just as Jack fired twice at Earl. The first bullet lodged in a doorframe; the second caught Thurmond in the back. He tumbled forward on top of Earl, causing Nelly to drop to the floor. Through the commotion, Nelly managed to crawl away and escape into another room.

The .45 caliber bullet ejected gunpowder, which burned though Thurmond's jacket and skin. It shattered his breast-bone and turned it into shrapnel, which propelled towards his heart and lungs. The shrapnel created a shock wave through Thurmond's body, which destroyed all tissue in its wake. The heart ruptured as the bullet traveled towards the spinal column before it ricocheted right and exited the body. It took his right shoulder blade and its surrounding tissue with it. The exit wound, much larger than the entry, gaped open. Thurmond's heart kept pumping, which caused a massive hemorrhage.

Although technically dead, Thurmond still had reflective breaths and heaved. Blood drained from his nose and mouth.

Thurmond grabbed Earl's coat collar and stared him dead in his eyes... "They was just like... me..." Thurmond crumbled to the floor.

. . .

Jack wailed as he shot wildly at Earl. A bullet grazed Earl's face as he dashed out the front door. Jack chased him outside and shot until his revolver was empty. Earl disappeared into the forest. Jack walked back inside the farmhouse and fell to his knees next to Thurmond.

THE STANDOFF

*E*arl mapped out a plan in his mind before he executed it. He would go in from the back, search for Nelly and drag her out a window if he had to. He knew that time was of the essence, as Jack would quickly move from grief to vengeance. Although he had killed Thurmond, he would blame Earl. However, just as Earl was about to make his first move, a car pulled up the driveway. Earl stepped back and hunkered down out of sight.

Sully and his men followed the farmhouse's driveway up to the main house. They stayed several yards back. They took note of the car parked outside.

"Yeah, this is it. See the stained glass? There it is," Tiny exclaimed.

. . .

"Don't you move," Sully demanded as his men pile out of the car.

Sully carried a tommy gun while the others carried revolvers. They approached the farmhouse with great care. Sully gestured for the driver to run around to the back of the house. Sully and his crew took a few steps onto the front porch. The front porch's creaks were thunderous. *So much for the element of surprise*, Sully thought.

One man peeked inside the home through the stained-glass window, however his view was obscured. He shrugged his shoulders. Sully gently grabbed the doorknob and pushed the door open a few inches before it hit up against something. The other man had his gun drawn as Sully put his back into opening the door up wide enough for them to pass through.

The body of Thurmond blocked the door. Sully and his man stepped over the body to come inside. They tried to avoid stepping in his pool of blood, but were unsuccessful. Sully squatted down and touched the blood with two fingers. "It's still warm." He turned Thurmond over to see bundles of cash, all blood-soaked. He stood while the other man cautiously moved towards the sitting room. Sully left bloody footprints as he walked towards the kitchen. He saw evidence of recent activity. He met the other man in the sitting room, where Nelly's bed of straw lay spread out. Rope hung from the heater.

.   .   .

The men walked together, side by side, down the hallway towards the bedroom. The door was ajar. Sully used the barrel of his tommy gun to open the door. Inside, Jack and Nelly stood close as he held a gun to her side. He had a tight grip on her arm.

Sully realized that he faced a delicate situation, and he was not going to let some crumb stand in the way of his big payday. "Easy, Mac. We ain't here for you, just the lady."

The look in Jack's eyes showed true fear for the first time. Yet he knew he still held the cards. "Who are yous? Lazia's puppets?" Jack mocked.

Sully smiled, "So you know of Lazia? Then you know it's over. Now I'll give you two choices. You can let Mrs. Donnelly go right now, and we'll let you walk out of here. Or you can blow her head off, in which case, we won't kill you right away... though you'll wish we had. When we're done with 'chew, your own mother couldn't identify the body. So what's it gonna be?"

Sully and his men had both barrels pointed at Jack, although they knew Mrs. Donnelly could still become a casualty from an unintentional stray bullet. Sully had no choice. Jack pulled Nelly closer and put a greater distance between them and Lazia's men. A wide smirk spread across his face. Sully had seen this response before when someone had made up their mind. Sully pointed the tommy gun directly at Jack's head.

· · ·

In a calm voice Sully said, "Don't do it, Mac."

Nelly was frightened, yet empowered, *This is my chance; probably my last one to do something. I will see my family again. I will not die today.* Nelly whipped her head back and broke Jack's nose with her skull. She immediately broke free from Jack and dropped to the ground. Jack grabbed his bloody nose. Infuriated, he cocked the hammer to his pistol and *BOOM.* Jack loosened his grip on his revolver and fell to the ground. He had a look of disbelief on his face before he collapsed right next to Nelly. The back of his skull had been blown to bits. The driver, who had made the kill shot, climbed into the bedroom from the open window. Blood splatters covered one side of Nelly's neck, yet she remained motionless. Sully removed his coat and placed it over her shoulders.

"We're taking you home," Sully announced as he helped Nelly to her feet and before he instructed both men to gather all the cash. He escorted Nelly from the farmhouse.

~

Outside, Earl waited with great anticipation. A feeling of relief showered over him once he saw Nelly exit the farmhouse. Nelly stopped in her tracks and turned towards the woods where Earl crouched. They locked eyes.

Sully's eyes darted over the grounds, "What is it? You see somethin'? You see the another one?"

· · ·

She sent her gaze away from Earl and simply said, "Just take me home."

The driver gestured for Tiny to get out of the car. Tiny followed the driver to the trunk of the vehicle where he popped the trunk, untied Tiny's wife, and helps her step out.

Sully handed Tiny a wad of dough. "Consider yourself paid in full for your services. Now beat it."

Tiny and his wife turned and walked down the long driveway towards the main road.

"Who are they?" Nelly asked.

"Nobodies," Sully responded.

Nelly was helped into the vehicle. Sully and his men piled in and started up the engine.

THE STARS

*H*arrison received a phone call from Paul telling him that Nelly was on her way home. He said that the call came from Senator Reed's office. Paul then asked for privacy, and Harrison agreed. He sent several uniformed officers to clear away the press. Sure it was a big story with a happy ending, but they would have to wait to get the full scoop. Harrison could place this one in the "win" column, although he was not directly instrumental in her rescue. He now had the location of the farmhouse and would personally see to the cleanup.

Bailey arrived and dropped a box on his desk. "For you, Captain Harrison. It's heavy too," Bailey offered as he shook the box near his ear.

"Who dropped it off?" Harrison asked.

· · ·

"Too chaotic at the desk. Must have slipped in and out," Bailey responded.

Harrison took the box as Bailey returned to his desk. Harrison noticed that there was no postage or return address. He cautiously cut the twine and opened the box. His revolver was inside with a note. The note simply stated:

You can thank me later.

~

The driver pulled up to Nelly's home. Sully jumped out and offered his hand to Nelly to assist her in stepping out. She accepted.

"I want to thank you —"

"No thanks necessary," Sully replied as he hopped back into the car.

Paul opened the front door as Sully and his men drove away. He couldn't believe his eyes. She was bruised, had lost several pounds, and had great difficulty walking, but it was her. His eyes swelled up with tears as he reached out to her. They embraced in silence for what seemed like an eternity. Both refused to let the other go. Nelly's legs buckled. Paul caught her and gently seated her on the porch swing. He sat next to her.

. . .

"How is my baby?" she asked.

"He's upstairs; asleep. His first night back actually. After this afternoon when you weren't at the second bonfire… I needed him here with me."

With anxiousness, Nelly said, "I have to see him."

Paul placed his hand under Nelly's arm and helped her stand up. He then picked her up the way a groom carries his bride over the threshold. He brought her inside and up the stairs to David's room.

∾

One month later, Nelly met with her attorney, James Taylor, in his office. She shut the door behind her and took a seat. Taylor was no good at hiding anything, including his shock at Nelly's appearance. Her gaunt frame told the story of her ordeal.

"You're looking well," he lied.

Nelly chuckled, "For a corpse? Please, James. You know I am not one for false flatteries."

. . .

Taylor put away the falsities, "I have to tell you, Nell. It didn't look good. Quite desperate, actually. What happened to you? Did they treat you honorably?"

Nelly cleared her throat, feeling a bit uncomfortable. "I am working diligently to put all bad thoughts and memories behind me, and that means not repeating the story ever again."

"Understood. So why did you want to see me?"

Nelly stood and walked over to the window to avoid eye contact. "I need you to draw up papers."

"Of course. What type of papers?" Taylor asked.

Nelly regained her inner strength to tackle this head-on. She turned and faced Taylor, "Divorce papers. I'm divorcing Paul. I also need to buy him out of the company. I don't want to barter, go back and forth. He'll receive generous compensation, more than he himself would ask for."

Taylor looked perplexed, "Are you sure about this, Nelly? Perhaps it's too soon to make such drastic decisions."

Nelly was unwavering, "It's what I want. What I've learned recently is that tomorrow is promised to no one. Paul will be free to pursue… other interests. It is what is best for both of us."

"Okay then."

There was a knock at the door before it opened. Senator Reed stood in the doorway.

Nelly smiled, "Senator Reed. I understand I have you to thank as well. I apologize that I haven't reached out in person sooner. I know my letter was not adequate enough. But I hope you understood."

Taylor walked out of his office and shut the door to give them privacy. Reed took a seat on the edge of Taylor's desk.

"I'm not going to ask how you are doing. That is quite evident," Reed remarked.

Nelly walked over to the desk, "You never gave up, did you? No matter the political repercussions, personal demands… you-saved-me," she said with raw emotion.

"I had a bit of help," Reed confided. "I take it you've kept up with the papers? For the last few weeks the headlines have been nothing but how a Senator worked with organized crime figures to free Kansas City's Nelly Don of the Nelly Donnelly Garment Company."

Nelly confided, "I've made it a point not to read the headlines. In fact, Paul cancelled our subscription to save me the —"

"Pain? That is quite admirable of him. How is little David?" Reed asked.

Nelly smiled simply at the thought, "He is wonderful. Simply perfect."

"I would like to see him, you know... still on your timetable of course," Reed requested.

"I believe it's time," Nelly stated.

Reed reached into his pocket and pulled out Nelly's letter that Sully gave him in the church.

"I didn't know you kept my letter with you," Reed shared.

"May I have it back?" Nelly asks. "It gave me strength when I needed it most."

. . .

Reed hands the letter back to Nelly. She griped it with intensity as she sobbed.

Reed reached out both hands and Nelly took them as he pulled her towards him. He whispered in her ear, "My heart stopped beating while you were away. And not speaking for a month after ... Oh how I do want to spend the rest of my days, under the stars, with only you."

They embraced. "I had to wait. You must understand. I had to make sure it was over for Paul and me. Paul had to want our separation as well. I couldn't leave him if he wanted to make it work." Nelly pulled away, "You should not have risked your career, your livelihood, your marriage, for me."

Reed stepped closer and held her face in his hands, "I refused to accept that all I would have left are memories. I don't regret *any* decision I made or *any* actions I took."

Reed wiped away her tears. He confided, "It took everything inside me not to see David while you were gone. Because I thought that he could be all that was left of you and me."

Nelly took Reed's face into her hands, "You have us both. That is a promise."

Reed kissed Nelly's upper lip, then lower, before a full-blown, no-holds-barred kiss. They had never kissed like this before: raw, consuming, unleashed. They refused to hold back this time. He was hers and she was his... forever.

THE END

AFTERWORD - NELL DONNELLY

Nelly Donnelly Reed sold her profitable company in 1956. She was colleagues and friends with Coco Chanel. She revolutionized the garment industry with affordable, stylish everyday wear. She also made sure every employee was paid above-average wages, had full healthcare and childcare, along with paid higher education. She lived to be 102 yeas old, passing away September 8, 1991. She never spoke of her kidnapping from the time of her rescue to her passing.

Nelly Don Original

AFTERWORD - SENATOR REED

Senator Reed stayed married to his wife until her death from an illness, a year later.

Nelly and Senator Reed married and raised their son, David, together for twelve years, before his death in 1944. Senator Reed caught pneumonia while fishing in the rain, and passed shortly thereafter.

AFTERWORD - PAUL DONNELLY

 Nelly divorced Paul and compensated him one million dollars for his share of the Nell Donnelly Garment Company. Paul re-married a younger woman, and they had a child together.

Unfortunately, Paul passed away before his child was born. Nelly stayed in touch throughout his illness. Paul left a substantial estate of over $500,000 to his new wife and child: an estate which distant relatives vied for.

AFTERWORD - JOHNNY LAZIA

Johnny Lazia was believed to have been involved in the infamous Union Station Massacre, along with Pretty Boy Floyd. Underworld rivals caught up to Lazia, and gunned him down in 1934, just outside his home. He saved his wife and driver by pushing her out of harm's way and waving them to drive off. He was rushed to St. Joseph's Hospital, where he held on for eight hours before succumbing.

AFTERWORD - TOM PENDERGAST

Tom Pendergast's end was not as dramatic. He was tried and convicted of federal tax evasion. After serving less than two years, he was free. However, in 1945, the reign of "Tom's Town" was over. He could no longer rule Kansas City with an iron fist; as he lost his influence. He died of a heart attack that same year.

WHAT DID YOU THINK?

Dear Reader,

I hope you enjoyed **The Abduction of Nelly Don**. I have to tell you, I really enjoyed writing with real people in mind. Although I had to fill in the gaps and create some drama here and there... I left the essence of the individuals intact.

Why do you think Nelly Don never spoke of the event again? I wish I would have had the opportunity to ask her.

Tell me what you liked, what you loved, or even what you hated. I'd love to hear from you. You can write me at pwm@patricewilliamsmarks.com or visit my website at: www.PatriceWilliamsMarks.com.

Finally, I need to ask a favor. If you're so inclined, I'd love a review of **The Abduction of Nelly Don**. Loved it, on the fence — I'd just enjoy your feedback.

As you may know, reviews can be tough to come by these days. You, the reader, have the power now to make or break a book. I hope you use your powers for good (*wink*).

Feel free to leave one on *GoodReads. For links to all other sites including Amazon, B&N, iBooks, Google Play, CLICK HERE to be taken to my site with direct links.*

WANT ORIGINAL NEWSPAPER ARTICLES/F.B.I. FILES on the Nelly Don Case? Join my newsletter list for exclusive giveaways only available to subscribers. Go to my website **home page** and click the **RED** button.

Thank you so much for reading my book and for spending time with me.

In gratitude,

Patrice Williams Marks

Website: www.PatriceWilliamsMarks.com
Facebook: Author.PatriceWilliamsMarks
Facebook: TheAbductionofNellyDon
Twitter: @PWilliamsMarks / Twitter: @Unfinished_The

ABOUT THE AUTHOR

Patrice Williams Marks penned her first book in third grade: The Day Snoopy Got Married. While it didn't make the New York Times Best Seller List, it was an instant classic with the Nunaka Valley Elementary School staff. From that moment forward, Patrice knew she was a writer. With a zest for travel and an insatiable appetite for all things vintage and period, Patrice uses her investigative journalism background to create authentic characters to occupy the pages of her books. Patrice has a talent for shining a light on riveting, obscure true stories from times past and generating page turners. Her series, **MONTGOMERY VALE**, follows this same successful formula.

www.PatriceWilliamsMarks.com
pwm@patricewilliamsmarks.com

BOOK #1 MONTGOMERY VALE, SCORCHED

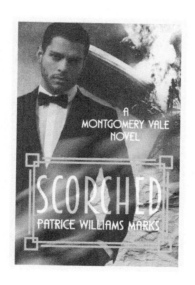

The year is 1937 and England's well-respected investigator, Montgomery Vale, is aboard the Hindenburg, determined to find answers about his family's mysterious past. But, an even more disturbing mystery derails him along the way.

Visit www.PatriceWilliamsMarks.com for purchase links.

MY LIBRARY

THE UNFINISHED

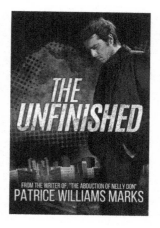

Another Film Noir Futuristic Thriller...

"I really liked this story from screenwriter Patrice Williams Marks. "The Unfinished" centers on a man brought back from the dead for 72 hours in order to identify his killer. It's written in a real conversational style, and builds up to a fun, surprising conclusion. I've already said too much." **Derek Haas, writer of films 3:10 to Yuma, Wanted, 2 Fast 2 Furious**

In a future where the Unfinished (murdered) are brought back to life for only 72 hours to testify against their killers before being "put down" for eternity, an Unfinished is resurrected to what he believes to be his one chance to point the finger at his accused killer.

He remembers the final details of his life; his boring job

as a mattress salesman, the dame he had high hopes for and the mug who took his life.

Once brought back from the dead and taken to court, this Unfinished could never have imagined what was awaiting him.

Set in a world that is our future, giving homage to 1940's detective noir stories, "The Unfinished" serves up a twist ending that will leave you wanting to follow his story to the end.

Made in United States
Orlando, FL
22 March 2022

16017144R00171